William Albrook   Nazar Alikhan   Thierry Allano   William Allen   James Allman   Marjorie Allthorpe-
up Consulting Engineers (Dublin)   J Ascher   Bruce Ash   Emily Ash   Zack Ashby   Al Ashe   Sarah
ephen Barry   Basildon Development Corporation   Peggy Bateman   e McCarthy
Attwood   Selje Aukland   Robert Axten   Nick Ayres   Alan Bacon   ce Bahouth
my   Alexander Beleschenko   Stefan Behnisch   Martin Benson   Ja   y Kathleen
s   Sean Billings   Billings Design Associates   David Bishop   Marga   isse   Katie Blach   Jeannette
icola Bone   Debbie Borst   Christopher Boulton   Manuel Bouza   Matthew Bowers   Michael Bradley
ridges   James Briggs and Partners   k Bris ee   British Rail   British Telecom
andy Brown & Associates   Mr an   Walter Buck   Building Design
s Burland   Buro Happold   Jonathon   on   Bim Burton   Mireille Burton
Calder   Carl Callaghan   Francesca Ca   ngs   David Cantwell   Cardiff Bay
r   Mervyn Carter   Karl Cashen   Hugh Casson   L   astle   Hilary Castle   Lorraine Caunter   The
eil Charles-Jones   Afial Chaudhry   Chichester Theological College   Richard Christmas   Peter Clapp
ld   Janet Cockerill   Lynn Cohen   Chris Cole   Clifford Cole   Rob Cole   Effie Collen   Lyal Collen   Rosie
  Catherine Cooke   Nicholas Cooney   Stuart Cooper   Tim Cooper   Nancy Copplestone   Athol Corbett
x   Sue Cracknell   Adam Craig   Michael Craig-Martin   Crest Nicholson   Janet Crickmay   Catherine
s Engine Co   Colin Cunningham   Mark Cuthbert   Dale & Ewbank   Michael Dames   Harry Danjahl
  Robert Davys   George Dawson   HL Dawson & Associates   DDE, Grenobles, France   Paul De Freine
& Partners   DEGW   Simon Dennison   Department of Education & Science, Ireland   Department of
  Desai   John Dewe-Mathews   Dewhurst McFarlane   DHSS, UK   DHSS Directorate of Development
n   Norman Dilworth   Sam Dingle   Keith Dixon   Lucette Dixon   Docklands Light Railway   Christopher
Paul Drake   Reuven Druckman   Sally Dryland   Dublin City Corporation   Dublin Dental Hospital   Frank
olin Eastwick   Richard Eastwick   Harriet Edgerley   Ian Edmundson   Alan Edwards   Kate Edwards
llis   Richard Ellis   Carlos Elsesser   Robert Emmerson   Engineering Design Consultants   Richard
elle Fagan   Fairclough Homes Ltd/Amec   Stephen Falvey   Ferguson & Partners   Anthony Ffrench-
od   Aaron Fletcher   Frances Fogarty   Max Fordham   Max Fordham and Partners   Foreign and
elle Francis   Nathan Freebury   Eddie French   Sally Freshwater   Elizabeth Frink   Richard Galbraith
& Theobald   Declan Garvin   Jackie Gately   Manuelle Gautrand   Glare Gerrard   Mark Gibson   Gifford
oldenberg   Andy Goldsworthy   Christine Goodliff   Howard Goodman   Michael Goold   Nick Gooney
  Walter Greenhill   Jane Greening   James Griffin   Mary Griffin   Mandy Griffith   Habitat   Bruce Haden
art Hampson   Richard Hankin   Hanscomb   Andrew Harding   Adam Hardy   John Harris   Matthew
son   William Harrison   Richard Harryott   Alex Hartley   John Hawkes   Darrell Hawthorne   Hayes
k   Martin Heffernan   Nicola Hem   David Hemmings   Bill Henderson   Filip Henley   Mark Hensmann
tt   Roger Hibberd   Peter Higson   Eric Hill   Stuart Hill   Matthew Hilton   Jane Hinton   Sophie Histon
an O'Brien Associates   James Hope   Simon Hornby   Richard Hough   Gordon House   John Howard
e Hughes   William Hughes   Maria Hugo   Undine Hugow   Howard Humphries   Tony Hunt   Anthony
Hutton   INPUT Pain Management   IBM (UK) Ltd   Bill Impey   Geoffrey Inkin   Institute of Technology
teven Jacobs   Tamar Jacobs   Edward Jakmauh   Stephen Jamieson   Tess Jaray   Jaros Baum & Bolles
ohnson   Penny Johnson   Johnson   on Drury Consultancy   Bella Jones   Canon
Esther Jury   Serge Kadleigh   J Kah   arvountzi   George Kasabov   Kasmai   John
Kennedy   Kent County Council   Douglas Keys   Tony Khan   Angela Kidner   Tony Kiley   Anne Killian
  Tom Knott   Mary Kong   Ben Koralek   Jenny Koralek   Lucy Koralek   Paul Koralek   Anna Koutelieri
sign   Landmark Practice   Barry Lane   Peter Langford   Langlands and Bell   Harvey Langston Jones
ractice   Mark Lecchini   Sally Ledger-Lomas   Frank Lee   Thomas Lee   Lee McCullough & Partners

Collaborations: The architecture of ABK

The architecture of ABK

Edited by Kenneth Powell

laborations

August – London

Birkhäuser –
Publishers for Architecture
Basel • Boston • Berlin

Contents

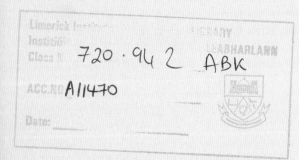
A CIP catalogue record for this book is available from the Library of Congress, Washington DC, USA

Deutsche Bibliothek Cataloguing-in-Publication Data Collaborations: the architecture of ABK / ed. by Kenneth Powell, – Basel ; Boston ; Berlin : Birkhäuser; London : August, 2002 ISBN: 3-7643-6644-3

ISBN 3-7643-6644-3

9 8 7 6 5 4 3 2 1

Printed in Spain

© 2002 August Media Ltd,
116–120 Golden Lane,
London EC1Y 0TL,UK

www.augustmedia.co.uk

© 2002 Birkhäuser – Publishers
for Architecture, P.O. Box 133,
CH-4010 Basel, Switzerland
Member of the
BertelsmannSpringer
Publishing Group

Printed on acid-free paper
produced of chlorine-free
pulp tcf ∞
Production co-ordinated by:
Uwe Kraus GmbH

Editor: Kenneth Powell
Authors: Elain Harwood,
Paul Finch, Frank McDonald,
Jeremy Melvin

Art direction and design:
Peter B. Willberg and Paul Baron
at Clarendon Road Studio
Project editor: Alex Stetter
Publishing Directors:
Nick Barley, Stephen Coates

Overview Kenneth Powell

"The Heroic Age of modern architecture is the rock on which we stand", wrote Alison and Peter Smithson in 1965. "Through it we feel the continuity of history and the necessity of achieving our own idea of order." The Smithsons were children of the 1920s, growing to maturity and beginning to practise architecture just as the Modern Movement in Britain took its place as one of the foundations of a new welfare state. For Peter Ahrends, Richard Burton and Paul Koralek, all born in the year of Adolf Hitler's assumption of power – the catastrophe which eventually brought Ahrends and Koralek to Britain – things could never be that simple. Ahrends, Burton and Koralek (ABK), the practice which the trio formed in the autumn of 1961, was to spearhead the rise of a new critical modernism which questioned many of the assumptions of the recent past. The radical, iconoclastic spirit of the Smithsons and the New Brutalism were, of course, formative influences on Ahrends, Burton and Koralek – Peter Smithson taught at the Architectural Association while they were students there. But ABK's architecture, though tinged by the Brutalist obsession with Mies van der Rohe and Le Corbusier, took a different course and over four decades has offered a vision of a pragmatic but poetic modern architecture in which the classic balance of form and content is given a new inflection by a recurrent preoccupation with place. Eschewing the universalist ambitions of High-Tech (and, even more clearly, the explicit historicism of Post Modernism), ABK's work has always been – as Peter Blundell-Jones has insisted – "decidedly empirical".[1] That empiricism is rooted in a genuine humanism: ABK's idea of order is human-centred, permissive rather than prescriptive, expressive to a degree, a celebration of the diversity of life. Amongst the work of modern British masters only that of the late James Stirling, perhaps, offers such a persuasive alternative to the enduring hegemony of High-Tech – the openness and unpredictability of ABK's response to any brief is equally characteristic of Stirling (who, born in 1926, was building the Ham Common flats while Ahrends, Burton and Koralek were completing their studies at the AA).

Christened "the country boys" by their contemporaries at the AA on account of their espousal of the cause of Frank Lloyd Wright, Ahrends, Burton and Koralek were content to be out of step. Peter Ahrends recalls being cheered by the approach of Arthur Korn (a much revered teacher): "In those days, everything was supposed to be rational – you weren't supposed to express emotions. But Arthur was hugely emotional – he believed that you should express your feelings in your work." The advice was taken to heart. Both Koralek and then Burton cut their teeth as young practitioners in the office of Philip Powell and Hidalgo (Jacko) Moya, who were loyal supporters of ABK in its early years and pioneers in their own right of a contextual modernism. Before joining Powell & Moya, Richard Burton had done a stint at the London County Council. "Point blocks were the order of the day", he recalls. Burton soon moved on. Some years later, asked to include a high-rise element in its Basildon housing, ABK refused point-blank, believing that few people wished to live in tower blocks. The

Basildon schemes became a landmark in the rise of sustainable housing design. Energy issues form a hugely important ingredient in the holistic approach, a search for "completeness", which Richard Burton sees as central to ABK's work from the beginning.

ABK's first significant built works, the Berkeley Library at Trinity College Dublin, and Chichester Theological College, both slotted into historic cities, exemplified the young firm's belief in digging deep into the physical and human context of any project. What greater contrast could there be between the varied and intimate spaces at

Trinity College, and the bland Miesian box of Sheffield University Library, designed by GMW, completed in 1959? Like ABK's school at Thurmaston in Leicestershire, the later extension to Keble College, Oxford, and indeed, the Trinity College arts faculty, Chichester is about "incidents on a route", private spaces enclosing and defining a more open, communal domain. Peter Ahrends traces back the contrast between the open and lightweight and the closed and more solid – the "hard back, open front" approach seen, for example, at Templeton College – to the very early Bryan Brown house in Devon

Berkeley Library, Dublin

(which he designed with Richard Burton) with its combination of heavy blockwork and transparent timber and glass. The same contrast is seen in the Maidenhead Library, where a lightweight space-frame roof, welded up and raised into position in one piece, presides over a "village" of highly specific spaces defined by the exposed brickwork which, externally, helps to connect the building to its context. The use of brick here, at Keble College, the Oxford chaplaincy, and in Chichester was a practical and contextual move, but also seemed to symbolise a certain balance between continuity and radical change: Maidenhead was seen as a bold statement about the role of the public library in the community and the future shape of "social" architecture.

By the early 1970s, the themes which were to permeate ABK's work to the end of the twentieth century had clearly emerged. Social, urban and environmental concerns were never far below the surface, but there was also a passionate interest in architectural form and a sure conviction that mere functionalism was a dead end. As avid readers of Louis Sullivan, Ahrends, Burton and Koralek were unlikely to parrot the "form follows function" mantra. (Koralek likes to cite Sullivan's *Kindergarten Chats* as a masterly exposition of the necessity for form in architecture.) In 1964, ABK, in a project led by Richard Burton, produced designs for what was potentially one of the most impressive British churches of the post-war era. All that remained of St Anne's, Soho, after the Second World War was the extraordinary tower by S.P. Cockerell. The dynamic incumbent, Fr. John Hester, resolved to rebuild the church in tune with the prescriptions of Vatican II and the Liturgical Movement. ABK's scheme provided for a luminous, double-glazed sanctuary – John Piper worked on designs for stained glass there – contained within a dense protective framework of metal mesh and set in a raised public square. An underground car-park would have underwritten the project, but the

Bryan Brown house, Devon

Templeton College Oxford: grounds

Maidenhead Library: space-frame roof

St Anne's Church, Soho: model

1.1

Public and private. One of Jerusalem's most important public buildings, the Dome of the Rock, is framed by the stone piers of this private house for Dr Nebenzahl.

potential developer pulled out, Fr. Hester moved to another parish and the scheme was abandoned. It remains one of ABK's (and the Church of England's) great unbuilt projects, not least for the innovative design of the active facades, incorporating a ventilation system.

By the 1970s, ABK, with an office of around 50 people, was critically acclaimed as one of the most creative and versatile of Britain's younger architectural practices. The firm had been considered for both the British Library and National Theatre commissions, lost out to more senior figures, and ended up with the huge new Post Office headquarters in the City as a consolation prize. (Enriched by

extensive research into energy provision and the needs of future users, ABK's scheme was equally progressive in urban terms, providing for the retention of the Post Office's imposing Victorian headquarters, but fell victim to spending cuts.) During the same year (1975), Foster Associates' Willis Faber headquarters at Ipswich, another example of progressive workplace design, was completed. Like Richard Rogers and Renzo Piano's Pompidou Centre, then nearing completion in Paris, and the forthcoming Sainsbury Centre, Willis Faber was widely identified as an example of 'High-Tech' architecture. High-Tech's preoccupation with creating serviced spaces adaptable to a wide range of operational

scenarios could not have been further removed from the concern of ABK to address the needs of individual human beings and locations made unique by circumstances of place and time. The Habitat complex at Wallingford (1972–74) seemed close in spirit to the recent work of Farrell Grimshaw, for example – Richard Burton admired the latter's block of flats in Park Road, north London. But the chief imperative in the scheme, which cost just £6 per square foot (£65 per sq. metre), was economy with style: hence the cladding of corrugated asbestos cement. But ABK's client, Richard Burton recalls, "was someone willing to pay the extra needed for architecture, rather than

1.1

building". The podium of dark brick, rooting the sheds to the land, was a device that Norman Foster or Richard Rogers would not have contemplated.

There were superficial High-Tech echoes too in several of ABK's projects, such as the Cummins Engines factory, Sainsbury's supermarket at Canterbury and even St Mary's Hospital on the Isle of Wight. Yet the dominant theme at Cummins was that of worker participation: the late Paul Drake (a partner of ABK from 1974 on) conducted a formidably intensive consultation exercise. The building was completed in 1983, yet there was none of the forceful expression of services seen in the almost exactly contemporary Inmos factory by Richard Rogers. For Peter Ahrends, team leader for the Cummins project and an instinctive political radical, style was hardly an issue, but it was vital that the factory responded to the needs of its users and this imperative was reflected in both plan and form. (The strongly expressed window bays, for example, provided a place for people to take a break and maybe play a game of cards.) At St Mary's Hospital, the low energy agenda was to the fore. The project was one of many fruitful client collaborations – in this case, with the late Howard Goodman of the Department of Health – which have happily punctuated the history of ABK and was notable too as a pioneering exercise in the integration of art and architecture. Only in the case of Sainsbury's does Paul Koralek concede an element of styling. The client sought a large, unobstructed retail floor plate, obtained via the use of a masted structure. The "gothic" look of the building, close to one of England's finest cathedrals, was, says Koralek, more than fortuitous – something of a struggle was anticipated in the planning process.

David Cruse, who first worked for ABK during his year out in 1972–73 and returned as a full-time member of staff in 1977, recalls the office in those years as "intense and hugely challenging. Architecture was seen as

Post Office HQ, London: site plan

Post Office HQ, London: model

Cummins Engines factory, Scotland

Sainsbury's, Canterbury

1.2

Situated on a reclaimed urban site in north London, the Burton house is shielded from the road by a high wall. The circular gate evokes a 'secret garden'.

1.3

Through the gate, with the front door of the house open, the heart of the house can be glimpsed. Here, a glazed room faces onto an inner courtyard.

something which really mattered". For Cruse, it was the open, inclusive approach of ABK which impressed – "you felt that modern architecture could progress, in a critical fashion, learning from its mistakes and engaging people in its future direction". No practice was better equipped to advance the cause of contextual modernism than ABK. After a period of recession and self-doubt, heightened by the rise of the conservation, community and ecology movements, modern architecture in Britain could be on the verge of a renaissance. Margaret Thatcher's assault on the public sector dismayed many, but the prospect of a commercial property boom offered potentially rich pickings.

The fact that ABK benefited so little from the 1980s boom was partly a reflection of the practice's lack of experience in the key sector of the time: speculative offices. But there was another factor – the denigration which it underwent from the Prince of Wales over the matter of the National Gallery. The Gallery needed a major extension – the idea of developing one on the vacant "Hampton's" site had been under discussion for decades. Now Environment Secretary Michael Heseltine was determined to see progress. In tune with the spirit of the times, he proposed that commercial developers should come up with proposals for the site which might incorporate a profitable office element but

also provide new picture galleries at no cost to the public purse. Both the potential developers (who would get the land for 125 years at a peppercorn rent) and their chosen architects should be reliable hands, able to produce a building of suitably high quality. For ABK, approached by developers Trafalgar House, the project was tempting. Indeed, the idea of a mix of uses, cultural and commercial, in one urban block was in line with their ideas on urban living. Moreover, Trafalgar House, which reportedly wished to locate its own headquarters on the site, was receptive to a sensitive approach which did not over-egg the office element. There was every prospect that ABK, with its known

1.3

feeling for context, would produce a dignified addition to Trafalgar Square and in May 1982, the firm and its client were put on a shortlist of seven teams (out of 79 preliminary submissions) invited to develop their initial ideas into actual designs.[2] The seven schemes were put on public exhibition at the National Gallery in August, attracting 60,000 visitors, a fifth of whom took the trouble to complete the questionnaires provided.

Apart from ABK's winning scheme, only one of those on the shortlist is remembered today, that by Richard Rogers. Of the rest, the Arup/Rosehaugh scheme promised the most intensive and profitable development of the site (60% of the total area was given over to offices), while SOM's undemonstratively Classical proposal reportedly found most favour with the Gallery's trustees, notably for the layout of its internal spaces. The Rogers scheme was notable not only for its strongly articulated architectural vocabulary, with a prominent tower echoing that of St Martin in the Fields across the square, but also for the explicit dichotomy it proposed between the gallery and commercial elements of the development. Rogers won more "first choice" votes from the public than anyone, but his proposals were also the most widely disliked – RIBA President Owen Luder's supposedly supportive comments, moreover, did Rogers no favours. On balance, ABK's scheme won the popular vote and the practice was invited to participate in a "run-off" with Arup and SOM. Its practical appeal was strong: the lowest development cost of any of the seven and a judicious balance of commercial and public space.[3] In December, 1982, ABK/ Trafalgar House was announced by Heseltine as the winner of the competition.

Peter Ahrends uses the adjective "quiet" to describe the 1982 National Gallery scheme. Rejecting the High-Tech expressiveness of Rogers and the bankers' Georgian of SOM, ABK sought an appropriate modern language for a major public building in one of the most prominent locations in London without attempting to hide away the offices: they

1.6

The main entrance to the
Nebenzahl house in Jerusalem.

were given generous areas of transomed windows looking out to the square. The great barrelvaults of the top floor galleries had a Kahnian resonance, which extended into their internal section, with its debts to the Kimbell Museum. The circular court ("an antechamber to Trafalgar Square", as Ahrends describes it) which formed part of a pedestrian route through to Leicester Square, was an echo of Aston Webb's Admiralty Arch at the top of the Mall. The court was capped by a curving gallery which formed the connection to William Wilkins' building. The National Gallery trustees, chaired by the late Lord Annan, were unhappy about this feature of the scheme, preferring more

conventional rectangular spaces. There was further pressure to revise the scheme from the Royal Fine Art Commission. At the end of 1983, ABK's triumph was looking distinctly compromised. The substantial redesign of the scheme to produce the requisite gallery layouts included the introduction of a tower, which was seen in some quarters as a borrowing from the Rogers scheme. (This is denied by Ahrends, who saw the tower as a move intended to connect the new building more clearly to the original Gallery, with its "pepper pot" turrets flanking the central portico and dome.) The effect of the changes was to intensify controversy over the scheme,

which was duly called in to public inquiry by the government.

The inquiry opened in April 1984, with the objections to the scheme led by the Greater London Council and Westminster Council. On May 30th, speaking at the RIBA's 150th anniversary dinner at Hampton Court – also the occasion for the presentation of the Royal Gold Medal to the Indian architect Charles Correa – Prince Charles launched his assault on modern architecture. He described ABK's National Gallery scheme as "a kind of vast municipal fire station complete with the sort of tower that contains the siren. A monstrous carbuncle on the face of a much-loved and elegant friend". The impact of the speech was

immediate, with extensive media coverage: it launched the Prince's career as an arbiter of architectural taste. In September, the new Environment Secretary, Patrick Jenkin, rejected the National Gallery scheme as "altogether inappropriate for this site of national importance". Early in 1986, it was announced that Robert Venturi and Denise Scott-Brown had been chosen as the architects of what had become the National Gallery Sainsbury Wing, with the commercial development now entirely dropped.

The outcome of the National Gallery saga seriously damaged ABK, not because the quality of its work was in doubt but because prospective clients feared that the Prince might again interfere in the planning process and derail, or at least delay, any project to which he took exception. "We were seen as being in decline", recalls Peter Ahrends, who soon found himself devoting half of his working hours to his teaching post at the Bartlett School. "It was the beginning of a rather blank period." The support of other architects, like Richard Rogers, who wrote to commiserate on the outcome of the planning inquiry, was reassuring but did not compensate for lost commissions. For David Cruse, the outcome was one of polarisation – "the prospects for a humanistic modernism, a sort of middle way, vanished". Given its high standing amongst leading British practices,

ABK might have expected, but did not receive, an invitation to participate in the 1986 competition for the redevelopment of Paternoster Square, the 1960s office precinct close to St Paul's Cathedral. The competition was won by Arup Associates with a stripped Classical scheme which might have seemed well calculated to appeal to the Prince of Wales – but the Prince lambasted the proposals, and they were duly abandoned. ABK was shortlisted for the high-profile competition for Stag Place, Victoria, and produced an outstanding proposal, a potentially superb piece of urban architecture embodying highly progressive ideas on servicing and social space. In this

1.7

1.8

1.7	1.8
Situated on a highly sensitive site in the Jewish Quarter of the Old City of Jerusalem, the stone facade of the Nebenzahl house blends into its surroundings without resorting to pastiche.	Views from the Nebenzahl building are extremely dramatic: each of its three private apartments contains roomy living areas, leading to a balcony.

project and that for a site at Shaftesbury Avenue, both designed in 1986, ABK showed its mettle as a generator of memorable architectural form. As British architecture polarised between all-glass High-Tech and stick-on Post Modernist styling, ABK designed facades which, firstly, were a rational reflection of the spaces behind them and, secondly, were conceived, in their careful balance of masonry and glazing, as a response to the climate and the noise and pollution of central London streets. Sadly, both the Stag Place and Shaftesbury Avenue schemes remained unbuilt.[4] Designs for buildings at Chiswick Park remained unrealised. "I think companies

like Stanhope felt that we lacked the detachment needed for spec office work", Richard Burton believes.

In fact, the 1980s saw the completion of a number of important ABK projects – Cummins Engine factory, the second phase of work at Portsmouth Polytechnic, St Mary's Hospital on the Isle of Wight, Sainsbury's at Canterbury, and the WH Smith headquarters at Swindon, for example. The latter project (1982–85, with an extension by ABK in the mid–1990s) involved yet another inspirational client collaboration, in this case with (Sir) Simon Hornby of WH Smith. The layout of the offices reflected a close study of progressive exemplars beyond

Britain, notably Herman Hertzberger's Centraal Beheer in Holland. The entire building was naturally ventilated, with exposed ceilings, effective insulation and sun-shading reinforcing a floorplan and a materials mix both calculated to ensure comfortable working conditions and notable energy savings. All of this was rare in the early 1980s. The landscape, developed with one of ABK's most valued collaborators, James Hope, was another important element in the project, while, with Simon Hornby's support, a number of artworks were commissioned for the building.

The successful integration of architecture, art and landscape (again by James Hope)

1.9

1.9
In the mid-1960s, five individual owners formed a group to build the Dunstan Road houses near Oxford. This photograph is taken from the public road.

1.10
From the communal interior courtyard, the Dunstan Road houses offer a radically different facade.

1.11
Interior spaces at Chalvedon, although completed to a very modest budget, place an emphasis on space and light common to many ABK interiors.

was a prime objective in the house which Richard Burton built for his family on a tight (19m x 15m) site in Kentish Town from 1986 onwards. The house is a place of calm and quiet in a densely developed inner-city area and the phased completion of the project over fifteen years has been a personal delight to Burton. But it also embodies a vision of dense, but green and healthy, low-rise, low energy cities which, Burton believes, can be fashioned out of the battered mess that is much of urban Britain. In 1976 Burton took on the role of energy coordinator for the RIBA. A year later, he became a trustee of the new school of craftsmanship which the woodworker John Makepeace (who had

worked on the furnishings of Templeton College in the 1960s and subsequently at Keble College) had established at Parnham, Dorset. Burton resigned his trusteeship in 1983 when ABK was asked to work on buildings for the trust at nearby Hooke Park. The project, developed in consultation with Buro Happold and Frei Otto, provided for teaching, workshop and residential buildings, constructed in a woodland setting out of timber grown on site – the thinnings which might otherwise end up as firewood or waste and which Burton describes as "captured carbon dioxide". Two buildings by ABK were constructed, with a further residential building by Edward Cullinan

Architects. There was nothing folksy or ruralist about the use of wood at Hooke Park – it was a response to a specific circumstance, and the material was used in a modern way. New jointing methods, partly based on NASA research, and the extensive use of computer models were integral to the project.[5] This was a good illustration of ABK's belief in appropriate technology: the approach to timber engineering at Hooke Park was no more "traditional" than that to steel and glass in the unbuilt Mary Rose Museum project of 1980 – which produced, incidentally, ABK's first encounter with the Prince of Wales, Patron of the Mary Rose Trust. (The dramatic form of the great glazed

Stag Place, London: competition entry

Hooke Park, Dorset: built from thinnings

1.10

1.11

tent intended to house the hulk of the recovered Tudor warship was at odds with the typical "heritage" style of the period.)

The first discussions about the new John Lewis department store at Kingston upon Thames took place in 1979. Constructed in 1986–90, this project embodies, to an uncommon degree, the themes and ideas which had marked ABK's work since the early 1960s. Paul Koralek recalls that the job came to the practice through the good offices of Sir Hugh Casson – "I think we were seen as experts at tackling awkward sites", he says. The site in question was close to Kingston Bridge, a rectangle of land between the existing Bentall's store and the river

Thames. To the south, the development would address the conserved historic core of Kingston. To the north, it faced a rather untidy area dominated by multi-storey car-parks. The issues of scale and materials had to be addressed in finding an appropriate language for the scheme. Even more pressing, however, were the planning complications attached to the site, which was due to be bisected by a new inner relief road. The road engineers proposed a curving carriageway. "One of the first things we had to do was persuade them that the simplest route between two points was a straight line", says Koralek. With the road configuration agreed, the strategy for the new building

could be developed. In essence, it was to wrap around the relief road, weaving below and above it, with parking and service areas in basements and 32,000 square metres of retail space bridging over the traffic. The geometry of the scheme is that of two squares. At ground and first floor, slightly awkward triangular spaces are the inevitable outcome of the intervention of the road, but the huge day-lit room above, with stepped terraces linked by escalators, is one of the most memorable of post-war British interiors.

As partner in charge of the John Lewis development, Paul Koralek was able to draw on the lessons of a series of earlier library projects where top-lighting had been a key

1.12

1.13

1.12
The austere outer wall of ABK's residential block for Keble College shields residents from the busy street.

1.13
In common with other projects, the interior courtyard at Keble is light and communal, forming a soft core inside the hard external shell.

1.13

1.14

1.16

1.15

1.17

1.18

1.14
In contrast to Keble College, ABK's school at Thurmaston is designed to blur the boundary between the public and private, using a glass entranceway.

1.15
Inside Thurmaston school, the assembly space is designed to encourage a close, communal atmosphere, while also letting in plenty of light.

1.16
At Keble, on the other hand, visitors are guided inside the residential block along an intimate brick pathway which pierces the glass facade.

1.17
Inside Keble, student social rooms are interspersed between the private study bedrooms with staircase access.

1.18
The glass walkway snakes its way along the length of the ground floor of the building, around the inner courtyard leading to the staircases.

1.19
Thurmaston school's circulation spaces are open, and visibly linked both to the outside, and to the classrooms.

ingredient, beginning with the Berkeley Library in Dublin and including, of course, the Maidenhead public library. The library at Portsmouth Polytechnic, begun in 1975, featured a three-storey stepped interior under a sloping roof incorporating areas of glazing calculated to provide generous natural light without excessive solar gain. (Koralek eschews the radical, but, in practical terms, problematic gesture seen in Stirling's Cambridge library, where the all-glass roof created serious problems of over-heating: "The idea of a roof implies for me a balance of solid and void", he insists.) A huge amount of study and testing went into the design of the Kingston roof – it exemplifies what Koralek

understands by the term "High-Tech", not a display of technical wizardry for its own sake but the rational use of technology to achieve a desired end. The real inspiration behind the John Lewis scheme was the memory of the great iron and glass store interiors of the late nineteenth century, like Bon Marché and Printemps in Paris. However, the building had to work not only as a successful retail space, but equally as a positive contribution to the variegated townscape of Kingston and it is in this respect, no less than in its internal qualities, that it succeeds triumphantly.

Brick had been common currency at ABK from the beginning. By the 1980s this basically noble material had become a staple

ingredient of the witless Post Modernist fashion of the period, used as a decorative coating to give some visual interest to very many bad buildings. ABK's use of brick at Kingston was far more considered. The external glazing of the store was restricted to office and other ancillary areas – in the sales areas, wall spaces were at a premium for display (and, in any case, department stores want people to look at the goods, not at the view). The brick cladding was used to break down potentially daunting areas of solid wall. Care was taken to make explicit the nature of the brick as a cladding on a concrete frame, expressed in the colonnades around the building, while the juxtaposition of masonry

Burton's wedding day in 1956.
(from left: Koralek, Burton, Ahrends)

Formation Jeremy Melvin

When Peter Ahrends, Richard Burton and Paul Koralek arrived for their first year at the Architectural Association in the autumn of 1951, they were confronted with a situation which could have been lifted from Molesworth – that irrepressible satire

of 1950s private schools which the AA to some degree resembled. Left-wing students from the higher years, distantly echoing Molesworth's penchant for "toughing up" new boys, presented them with a petition calling for the reinstatement of Robert Furneaux Jordan, the principal who had been forced to resign over the summer. The

with lightweight steel and glass elements is a typical ABK tactic. The infill panels of square bricks could be seen as a decorative device, but were integrated into the overall grid of the facades along with the window openings.[6] From the bridge, the building reads as a highly dynamic composition which balances light and solid elements and makes a strong contribution to the riverside scene. (Comparison with Quinlan Terry's slightly earlier Richmond Riverside scheme, designed for a very similar location only a few miles downstream, is instructive.) The final touch is provided by the semi-circular pavilion, with brick-clad columns encasing a glazed drum, which marks the main entrance to the store. This is a highly formal gesture, a nod to the civic dimension of the scheme, if slightly at odds with its prevailing mood.

Koralek remembers John Lewis Partnership – a company where the staff are known as "partners" – as a very special client. Its loyalty to ABK during the difficult years of the mid 1980s was precious. But there were comparatively few blue chip commercial clients of the stature of John Lewis Partnership, WH Smith and Cummins, and the public sector work which had always been the mainstay of the office was in increasingly short supply. Surprisingly, perhaps, given the dominant free market ethos of the period, there were infrastructural projects to bid for. The London Docklands Development Corporation, established by Michael Heseltine, had constructed the Docklands Light Railway (DLR) into the Isle of Dogs and in 1987 began planning the DLR extension to the Royal Docks. ABK was surprised (given its lack of experience in the field of transport), but delighted, to be approached to compete for the design of the eleven new stations on the extension, a £280 million project completed in 1993. The basic format of the line had been established by engineers Maunsell. The stations had to be straightforward, relatively economical, with a "kit of parts" which could be adapted to a number of distinct scenarios – stations on

1.20
The Arts Building at Trinity College Dublin. This student study area is a pivotal space in the building.

petition was unsuccessful, but each of Ahrends, Burton and Koralek remember it; this otherwise insignificant event introduced them to the character and contradictions of the AA, and provided the longest-lived three-way partnership in British architectural history with its first directly shared experience.

As they progressed through the AA far more significant events forged their relationship, and uncovered their latent interests which drew them together. The AA was then without doubt the leading architectural academy in Britain, and the early 1950s was a time when Britain made an unusually significant contribution to Modernist architectural thought. Several of the trio's tutors, like John Killick and especially Peter Smithson, contributed significantly to these developments.

Numerous contemporaries, including Ted Cullinan who joined their cohort from Cambridge in the fourth year, Cedric Price who followed the same route a year later, and Richard Rogers who was a few years junior to them, evolved particular and personal positions within this milieu. This chapter sketches Ahrends', Burton's and Koralek's passage through the AA and identifies how some of their experiences in the school

1.20

viaducts, island stations and those contained within traffic roundabouts. There had to be provision for extension when passenger numbers grew. A series of components was developed, with services neatly integrated into structural members. The aesthetic of the stations was one of lightness and transparency – the latter was seen as vital on a largely unmanned system – and there are echoes, for example, of Sainsbury's, Canterbury. Colour was used sparingly (for example, on lift shafts), in contrast to the Union Jack livery of earlier DLR stations.[7] On the basis of its work on the DLR, ABK was commissioned in 1993 to design four new stations (at Haggerston, Dalston Junction,

Hoxton and Bishopsgate) for the proposed extension of London Underground's East London Line. The project, however, fell into limbo and when revived early into the new century there was no mention of the involvement of ABK (or, indeed, any other architect). ABK's unified approach to the design of these new rail systems was in tune with that of London Underground in the heroic inter-war years. The practice was not necessarily in sympathy with the very different strategy adopted, under the leadership of Roland Paoletti, for the Jubilee Line Extension. There were discussions, and talk of possible involvement with London Bridge, but, in the end, no commission.

Simple cost-cutting, which undermined so many public projects of recent years, derailed the proposed Eurostar depot designed for a site alongside the main line out of Paddington. A cheaper design-and-build scheme was substituted.

If there were some disappointments for ABK during the 1980s, winning the commission in 1988 for the new British Embassy in Moscow (Foster & Partners and Arup Associates were also shortlisted) was a landmark in the history of the practice, confirming its standing at the top of the British profession.[8] British diplomats were working in distinctly substandard conditions, crammed into the Kharitonenko Mansion,

1.21

1.21
From the inside, Redcar Library is a large, democratic open space with generous lighting and even the odd Bertoia chair thrown in.

1.22
Redcar's exterior revels in a clearly articulated roof structure which extends to become an entrance porch, inviting the public in from the street.

1.23
The huge steel roof girders allow for jokes such as this means of bringing extra light and roof height into a coffee bar and exhibition space.

Koralek, Ahrends and Burton with their partners in 1979

helped to form their approach to architecture.

The seeds of their relationship germinated early. Under the benign eye of the first year master, Leonard Manasseh and his assistant Olive Sullivan, their first project was that perennial favourite way of breaking students into architectural education, the primitive hut. Koralek remembers being very impressed by Burton's, just about the first time that they began to notice something which appealed in each other's work.

Koralek may also have intuited something

of his colleague's background. For someone who had no architects among his immediate relations, Burton had grown up about as close to the heart of English modernism as possible. His grandmother, Christabel Burton (née Harmsworth) had commissioned F.R.S. Yorke to design his first house, Torilla, in the grounds of the family home outside Hatfield in 1934. A few years later Burton's stepfather Gerald Barry, who as editor of the *News Chronicle* had organised the famous school design competition of 1937, used the same

architect to remodel his cottage in Sussex. In one space in that house, a spectacular, double height, curving conservatory hung with a Marion Dorn rug and known as the elephant room, Barry had planned the Festival of Britain with its design director Hugh Casson and numerous artists and designers who contributed to it. Manasseh himself designed the '51 Bar' and won the student section of the schools competition. If that was not enough to imbue Burton with a confident veneer, his old headmaster from

an impressive town house, across the Moscow River from the Kremlin, ceded to the British after they recognised the Soviet Union in 1931. For many years, the Russians had been trying to persuade Britain to relinquish the mansion and move the embassy to a new location. A site a kilometre or two away, on Smolenskaya Embankment, long used as a timber market and sandwiched between two mammoth Stalinist blocks, was offered. From the start, it was obvious that the project would be fraught with problems. The Cold War may have thawed, but Russia was still a communist state, the hub of what Margaret Thatcher regarded as "an evil empire". ABK's first scheme for the Smolenskaya site was

security-driven, and a compact building, with all the accommodation contained under one overarching roof, was proposed. "There was also the issue of how on earth we were going to get it built", says Richard Burton, who led the project from the start. The new US Embassy had ended up badly constructed and riddled with electronic "bugs". Fortunately, ABK was never called on to build its original scheme (which had received planning consent). With the collapse of communism, a new brief was developed under future ambassador Sir Andrew Wood and Mark Bertram, head of the Foreign Office estates department, a reflection of more cordial relations between Britain and Russia.

Even under the new regime, there were a number of practical obstacles in the path of the project: construction did not begin until 1996, and the building eventually opened in 2000. For ABK, it tested every assumption which had underlain the practice's work since 1961. Firstly, there was the issue of context, always to the fore at ABK. The building needed the scale to make its presence felt alongside its ornate and bulky neighbours. Its materials should be appropriate and pay some regard to Russian traditions (as well as the Russian climate) – the history of the site as a timber yard suggested one ingredient of the mix. But the building equally had to express something of

British Embassy, Moscow: second stage   British Embassy: computer rendering

the character of Britain and be a showpiece for British talent. One of its functions was to coordinate Britain's ever-expanding export drive in Russia. It should have dignity without pomposity: it was to be both a workplace and, for a number of staff and their families, a place to live (although the ambassador's official residence, it was agreed, should remain in the Kharitonenko Mansion). Burton was determined that other longstanding ABK preoccupations – landscape and the integration of art into architecture – should be reflected in the project, where he believed both to be essential. The building should embody that holistic view of architecture which Burton had always espoused. Perhaps

it was Burton's own Russian ancestry which drove his wish to make the building a fusion of Russian and British themes, in its own way a symbol of the erosion of so many years of suspicion and enmity.

It is in this respect, perhaps, that the building's most obvious success lies. The familiar image of Moscow is one of monumental scale. The embassy does not attempt to rival the scale of its neighbours on Smolenskaya Embankment. But in the modest streets behind the building, where the scale is much smaller, there are faint memories of an older Moscow, a medieval city, largely of timber, to which the language of the building, light and open, obliquely

refers. Monumentality is eschewed: from across the river, the embassy is seen as a group of four linked buildings, three of them containing staff apartments, a strategy which makes optimum use of views and daylight. The richly articulated facades reflect the close attention paid to shading and climatic control. On Protochny Street, where all entrances (for visitors, visa seekers and residents) are concentrated, use of "Moscow yellow" render, punctuated by panels inscribed with snatches of poetry from Russian and British authors, further roots the building to its setting.

Only privileged outsiders will penetrate to the interior of the embassy – most Russians

1.24

1.24
This 'hole in a wall' provides a new entrance to Trinity College Dublin. It is described by ABK as one of their most important strategic gestures.

get no further than the visa section – but it is inside the complex that the ideas behind the project really emerge. The notion of the route as the focal point of a building has been present in so many ABK schemes that its emergence here is no surprise: from the impressive entrance hall, a stair leads up to a large space adaptable for lectures, exhibitions or social events. This is the limit of access for most visitors, but from here a "long gallery" extends across the site, connecting all the buildings, linking private and more public areas – shades of the Chichester theological college, 40 years ago. Perhaps the embassy should be understood as being, like a college, a community, a place with communal and personal spaces balanced against each other, its heart the "cloister" of the central garden (once again designed by James Hope). It is a place capable of being self-sufficient, but also able to welcome the outsider and engage him in the culture which it symbolizes. With an exceptionally supportive client, Burton was able to break the mould of civil service thinking about buildings. He got the landscape and the art and created a building which actually seems to be loved by those who use it. That, if nothing else, says something to the Russians about the strength of modern architecture in Britain.

The later 1980s and 1990s generated other projects. Paul Koralek was the key player in the development of the Dover Heritage Centre from 1988 onwards, a scheme where the heavyweight and the transparent were counterpoised with particular elegance in a scheme which also refurbished a group of existing listed buildings. In Cardiff, Koralek served as a member of the Cardiff Bay Development Corporation's design panel and put his famous skills as a brief-writer to work in the ill-fated opera house competition. ABK did one building in the regenerated docklands, "a fun palace with a serious mission", as critic Martin Spring described the Techniquest science exploration centre.[9] The core of the building is a Victorian repair

1.25

1.25
The hole in the wall featured on the previous pages gives access directly into the Arts Building, with immediate access to its art gallery and study library.

1.26
Continuing directly through the Arts Building, the route leads into the centre of the Trinity College campus.

Bryanston, Mr Coade, turned up in their first term at the AA to talk about art in education. Bryanston was at the time one of very few English public schools to take art and craft seriously: Terence Conran was slightly older and John Donat an exact contemporary who entered the AA at the same time.

All this contrasted strongly with Koralek's experience, coming from Aldenham, a minor public school just north of London. Unusually it was his chemistry master who introduced him to modernist culture, occasionally locking the lab door and playing gramophone records of Stravinsky. Only one contemporary, remembers Koralek, went into the construction industry, and none into architecture itself. Unlike Bryanston, Aldenham offered little encouragement to cultural interests; it was Koralek's long habit of drawing houses which suggested to his family that he might become an architect, and an architect family friend who strongly advised going to the AA. Koralek's father approved the choice of career; he wanted his son to enter a respectable profession and, coming from Vienna – the family arrived in Britain in 1938 – he might just have felt slightly more positive about the respectability of architecture than a conventionally British bourgeois parent of the time. Koralek's cosmopolitan background and the AA's percipience had combined fruitfully; he had been offered a place in the previous year, but strongly urged to defer it. The interval gave him an opportunity to live in Paris and take a course in French culture at the Sorbonne.

1.26

shed, a remnant of the historic port which ABK was asked to incorporate in the scheme. The iron-framed shed was retained as the principal display space of the centre, "a dazzling, cathedral-like hall, bathed in daylight", as Spring described it, with other functions housed in new extensions. There are views out through the glazed south elevation to the bay.

ABK's extraordinary success in Ireland during the 1990s and into the new century partly explains the practice's relatively low profile in Britain in recent years.[10] It did not help that the most significant work to be

completed by ABK for some years, the Moscow Embassy, was far from Britain and seen by few architects or critics. Forty years into its history, however, ABK is well-equipped to re-engage with its roots. To an uncanny degree, the issues on which it focused three decades or more ago – energy and the environment, user participation and historic context – have become central concerns for architects in the early twenty-first century. The belief that buildings should reflect a holistic view of humanity, addressing far more than purely functional needs, is no longer considered eccentric.

ABK was launched on the architectural scene with a building, the Berkeley Library, which drew on the riches of the American architectural culture. For more than four decades, ABK has waged war on complacency by never doing the obvious – its relentless exploration of technologies and materials has a parallel on the global scene in the work of Renzo Piano. And it is in a world context that its architecture deserves to be seen: there is nothing parochial about ABK. Yet there is also a degree to which much of the work has a Britishness – more specifically, an Englishness – which locates

1.27
The project for St Anne's Church, Soho, takes a derelict site in central London and provides a transparent public space in the heart of the city.

1.28
The building's glass structure sits within a lightweight steel lattice. Light levels within the building would dramatically affect its exterior character.

1.29
The bold space frame roof over Maidenhead Library is designed to offer an all-embracing, anti-institutional welcome to the public.

Like Koralek, Ahrends arrived at the AA through the recommendation of a family acquaintance, and had also fled Nazi-occupied Europe with his family in 1937. But there the similarities in background end. Ahrends comes from a strongly architectural family. His father and paternal grandfather were both architects; the latter, Bruno, had been a founder member of the Ring, one of the most influential groups of radical architects in Berlin in the early 1920s, which put him close to the centre of that dramatic

crucible of modernity. He designed at least one modernist Siedlung and a number of white bourgeois villas in affluent Berlin districts such as the Wannsee, where the family lived. The traumas following the rise of the Nazis deprived Peter of this influence. As a four year old, he and his parents left for Johannesburg, where his father established a successful practice specialising in large domestic projects which owed little to his modernist heritage. It was a British employee of his father's, Mike Smith, who after

returning to the UK strongly recommended that Peter should study at the AA.

Meanwhile Ahrends' grandparents had left Germany to travel in Italy in the wake of Kristallnacht. After receiving a telegram advising them not to return to Berlin, they made for Britain, and even influential friends and strong backing from the RIBA's refugees committee could not save Bruno from internment. (He put his time at the Hutchinson Camp on the Isle of Man to good use, helping to establish what amounted to a university

it in space and time. The Keble College extension, the Burton House or John Lewis at Kingston are as English as the best of Butterfield or Hawksmoor (or Stirling). A profound understanding of space and time, indeed, underpins the achievement of ABK and it is this which deserves to be celebrated and revisited as we await the next moves from this outstanding practice.

1 Peter Blundell-Jones, introduction to *Ahrends Burton and Koralek* (Academy Editions, London 1991, p. 7).

2 The other architect/developer teams on the list were: Spratley & Cullearn/Barratt Properties; SOM/London Land; Sheppard Robson/London & Metropolitan; Covell Matthews Wheatley/ London & Edinburgh Trust; Arup Associates/Rosehaugh; Richard Rogers Partnership/Speyhawk.

3 For an analysis of the commercial content of the seven schemes, see F. Duffy, B. Williams, M. Fordham, "Inside story: office variations without a theme", *Architects' Journal*, 15 September 1982, pp. 60–63.

4 The various proposals for the Stag Place site are discussed and illustrated in "Unbuilt London", *Architectural Review*, January 1988.

5 See R. Burton, M. Dickson, R. Harris, "The use of roundwood thinnings in buildings – a case study", *Building Research & Information*, 26 (2), March/April 1998, pp. 76–93.

6 For an explanation of the philosophy of the cladding design see "Brick: special supplement", *Building Design*, September 1990, pp. 16–21.

1.29

1.30

1.31

1.30
The interior space is left dramatically open beneath the space frame roof but, within this volume, an upper floor is created for quiet study.

1.31
Next to the main lending library on the ground floor, intimate spaces such as this children's library are created.

and producing an inventive design for the reconstruction of Douglas. See Klaus Hinrichsen's paper on the subject.) Only after the war ended in 1945 did they reach South Africa, but Bruno died in Cape Town in 1947 before Peter had a chance to meet him again. Though this family connection to modernist architecture had become extremely tenuous, several years into his time at the AA it would result in a twinge of familiarity. A tutor sidled up to him and said in an accent which he might just have recognised as *echt Berlin*,

"Ahrends? Ahrends? I know zis name." It was Arthur Korn who had been a fellow founder of the Ring, and whose teaching, especially his third year course analysing urban history, would influence each of Ahrends, Burton and Koralek.[1]

Several common threads emerge in these three disparate backgrounds. Each had an appreciation that the world was wider than the limits of the AA or even London, though it was Burton, the most cosmopolitan but least travelled of the three, who found the

AA slightly disappointing. He did find a palliative through another family connection – his mother was Vera Russell, a formidable operator in the art world – he studied part-time with William Coldstream at the Slade. Koralek remembered being treated as an adult at the AA; for Ahrends, it was "a new world opening" after the vague disquiet he had felt in Johannesburg, and his first impression of London as he stepped off the boat train some weeks earlier, "black, grimy, chimneyed – remarkably grey and dark".

7 John Welsh, "Station masters", *Building Design*, 26 March 1993.

8 For the history of the project see J. Melvin, *The New British Embassy, Moscow* (London, Foreign & Commonwealth Office, 2000).

9 M. Spring, "Light entertainment", *Building*, 21 July 1995.

10 For an account of the Irish projects, see Frank McDonald's contribution to this book, p. 101.

The quotations from Peter Ahrends, Richard Burton, Paul Koralek and David Cruse are taken from conversations with the author conducted during 2000–01.

The author is grateful to Thomas Muirhead and Jeremy Melvin for their advice and inspiration and to the partners of ABK for expounding their work so vividly.

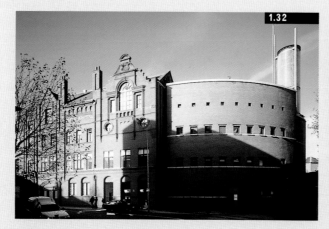
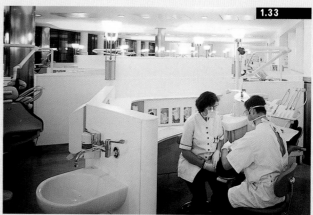

Whatever the different reactions, it was through – despite as well as because of – the AA that Ahrends, Burton and Koralek began to make common cause. The AA provided the common frame around which their different reactions started to form into a working relationship.

With their varied though interweaving personal experiences, this framework gradually assumed a rich pattern. They were each exposed in varying degrees to some version of modernist culture before entering architectural school. But importantly that experience was less direct and more complex than say, young Chitty in the year ahead of them whose father Anthony Chitty was the AA's president and a former partner in Tecton, nor did they emerge as stars in their year until close to the end of the course: John Toovey, later to be a noted zoo architect, and Barrie Dewhurst seemed to share the bulk of early year prizes. Ahrends, Burton and Koralek intuited something of modernism, but interpretations were not offered on a plate; they had to work out their own. For Koralek, this experience, if it can be measured at all, was osmotic, through being in Paris and attending the Sorbonne at a time of great intellectual excitement in the French capital. For Burton, this came through an experience of inhabiting modernist buildings and meeting modernist architects and artists.

Ahrends' experience was perhaps the most complex of all. Johannesburg of the late 1940s, where he came to maturity,

1.34

1.32
Set within the Trinity College campus, the facade of the Dublin Dental Hospital takes careful account of the older building which adjoins it.

1.33
Inside the Dental Hospital, a bright open space at the upper level is divided into a series of semi-private treatment suites for use by students.

1.34
A top-lit three-storey atrium enhances the impression that the building is open and publicly accessible.

1.35

The interior of the John Lewis store in Kingston dramatically balances light with a clear circulation route, to create a vibrant retail space.

When I was running Habitat, we wanted to build a warehouse, offices and a shop on a three acre site we had acquired opposite our existing warehouse in Wallingford, Oxon.

I was determined that we should build something that reflected the style of Habitat, my managing director who had had some building experience favoured a rather safe but dull approach of erecting an off-the-peg warehouse. After some rather heated debate, we eventually agreed on a budget which took the cost of a system warehouse and added 20 per cent to allow for the employment of an architect to design a building that was a bit special. We interviewed about six different firms and eventually settled on ABK because of the quality of their work and their enthusiasm to work within a tight budget. Coincidentally I had been at Bryanston School with Richard

Burton, which had no influence on our decision but made communication easy as we had seen and experienced many of the same things.

A lot of constructive discussion produced a final brief and a budget before design work started. ABK's presentation was outstanding and we accepted a design that answered all our practical requirements and fulfilled our aesthetic dreams. We were particularly excited by the ingenious steel structural solution that supported the roof and gave the warehouse virtually column-free space. I also liked the mezzanine office which prevented the warehouse from being segregated from the head office and allowed the buyers to see their overstocks!

The shop was a freestanding building with a children's playground with Paolozzi sculptures which looked like a spaceship, excellent planting

and a crinkle crankle wall dividing the loading bays from the public space.

A lot of discussion surrounded the colour of this giant ribbed structure until somebody ran into the back of my green Porsche and I had to have the engine cover replaced. Richard saw the damaged cover in my office and we agreed that the Jolly Giant as the Wallingfordians called it, should be green and the shop gleaming white.

The whole complex worked well, was built more or less to budget, received lots of awards, especially for its structural steel structure and was called "the finest barn in Oxfordshire". I think Richard's namesake Decimus Burton – not to mention Inigo Jones – would have liked it too.

Terence Conran

1.36

Terence Conran commissioned ABK to design an early Habitat store in 1972. Intended to provide a day out for the family, the showroom anticipates IKEA.

1.36

habitat

1.37

It was unusual at the time, but the provision of a play space and a Paolozzi sculpture at the Habitat store now seems unsurprising.

1.38

Together with a shop, Habitat required a warehouse space. The articulation of the volumes masks the fact that it is ten times larger than the shop.

1.39

Situated in Cardiff Bay, Techniquest is a discovery centre for children. Its mood is somewhere between playground and classroom.

displayed some of the most intense characteristics of the sense of modernity which Marshall Berman describes in *All That is Solid Melts into Air*. South Africa had emerged from the Second World War in a very strong position; it was, by some measures, one of the richest national economies in the world. But South Africa followed a different path to the British Labour Government (1945–51), which actively sought to redistribute the country's remaining wealth, or the United States, where economic

expansion continued into peacetime, giving even manual workers an undreamed-of standard of living. After its election victory in 1948 the National Party fiercely enshrined this inequity along racial lines through the policy of apartheid. Johannesburg, despite being less than a lifetime old and already on its third rebuilding, was by far the largest and richest city in the country; it was also the most ethnically diverse and culturally interesting. Not surprisingly, apartheid attracted widespread opposition, from white

intellectuals, a group greatly enlarged by refugees from the Nazis who had arrived in the previous ten years, and black activists, which included people of the calibre of Nelson Mandela and Oliver Tambo.

Much of this passed Ahrends by. Even before he reached Johannesburg, his personal identity had become subsumed in greater political events. His "agnostic, possibly atheist parents" had him baptised a Catholic in the belief that this was the best way to avoid the discrimination against

1.40
The foyer of the Dover Heritage Centre. From here, visitors can access a theatre and a glazed space which overlooks 'archaeological gardens'.

1.41
The first proposal for an extension to the National Gallery in London, this building had to accommodate commerce as well as art.

1.42
John Lewis in Kingston features a glazed entrance volume which faces towards the town centre. It hints at the unusual openness to be found inside.

1.43
Smaller structures which surround the vast main body of the John Lewis building are designed to relate to the scale of nearby buildings.

1.44
The entrance to St Mary's Hospital, Isle of Wight – a bridge between public and private worlds.

Jewishness. Once they reached South Africa, his parents, he remembers, despite their exposure to the Avant Garde and a short sojourn in the Soviet Union with Ernst May, "closed down". Perhaps the immediate family circumstances created enough disquiet. After their divorce in 1944, Ahrends' parents sent him a thousand miles away to a private school in East London, from which he was expelled after he succeeded at a second attempt to run away during Sunday chapel. Back in Johannesburg, his father's

glamorous lifestyle and numerous young woman friends caused some anxiety, and Ahrends developed an unease which the political situation intensified without crystallising it into an overt consciousness. Living in the affluent suburbs of Johannesburg with a father whose work rarely took him out of such areas, and educated at the city's exclusive King Edward's School, Ahrends, along with most white South Africans, could ignore the intense social cauldron of their country

without undue effort. A year as an apprentice on buildings sites gave him what political insight he had and he remembers realising that "I had to get away". There was a sense of enormity, restlessness and the lack of absolutes which can be read quite literally in some of his design work. After an initial shock at his son's reluctance to study in South Africa, Ahrends' father became very supportive. In 1951, Ahrends travelled up the east coast of Africa through the Suez Canal to Venice, where he had his first sight of

1.45

Poplar Station, on the DLR line in east London, combines a light rail station and a public footbridge across one of the busiest roads in the area.

Early Work Elain Harwood

In June 1961 Paul Koralek won an international competition for a new library at Trinity College Dublin, out of 218 entries from 29 countries. He announced that he would develop the scheme in conjunction with Peter Ahrends and Richard Burton, who had just

1.45

opened an office in London. The Berkeley Library at Trinity College was not quite the start of the practice, but it was an exceptional advent for so young a trio. ABK prospered in the 1960s on the public commissions common to the best firms then. But whereas the older elite of architects, particularly Powell and Moya, Chamberlin, Powell and Bon, and Howell Killick Partridge and Amis, had first built up their practices with low-budget schools and housing during the 1950s (the partners of HKPA did so while working for the London County Council), ABK came in at the top with their prestigious university win. The schools and housing were to follow in the less propitious 1970s. This section charts ABK's successes of the 1960s and 1970s, and shows how, unlike their peers,

Trinity College Dublin: campus

Berkeley Library, Trinity College: plan

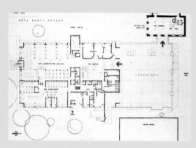

Berkeley Library, Trinity College

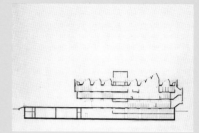

Trinity College Arts Building

1.46

1.47

1.46
An office and residential tower in Tel Aviv.

1.47
Design for the platforms of DLR stations in London.

1.48
Entrance to the Dover Heritage Centre.

Europe since he was five. He then made his way to the AA in London.

Vicarious exposure both to the intellectual modernism of Berlin in the 1920s and the experiential modernity of Johannesburg gave Ahrends a mass of unshaped material which at the AA began to interact with Burton and Koralek. Each of them brought a relationship to modernism which was not quite of modernism; together these relationships formed a framework that had notable affinities with modernism but also some detachment from it. They would never be uncritical of modernism, nor fall easily into simplistic categories. Quickly they began to work together on group projects, and after a few times realised that they were more effective as a trio, though they did form lasting associations with others. John Donat took memorable photographs of numerous buildings. Having Felix Samuely as a structures tutor led to a lasting relationship with Samuely's firm and its guiding force after Samuely's early death, Frank Newby.

Even external examiners fell under the spell. Philip Powell, despite having vowed never to employ AA graduates – as one himself, he knew their shortcomings more than most – offered a job on graduation to Koralek, who designed some houses at Swindon hospital. After Koralek went to work in Paris and New York, Burton took over. It was Powell who recommended them for the Chichester Theological College, their second project.

One shared interest they discovered early was Gothic. Koralek's family holidays had

they made the transition during the 1970s from public to private projects. Parallel to this shift, though not directly related, is a transition from concrete and brick towards a lighter aesthetic based on steel.

Koralek had worked for Powell and Moya on their Wythenshawe and Swindon hospitals, before setting off in 1959 to work in Paris, Toronto and thence the United States. When he won the Trinity College competition, he was working in New York for Marcel Breuer. Being in America gave him the then still rare opportunity to see the work of Frank Lloyd Wright in the flesh, particularly his early work in Chicago and Oak Park, as well as Taliesin and Fallingwater. It is striking to realise now that it was ABK's generation who "rediscovered" Wright – after the architect's

1.48

practice had slumped in the 1920s, his work only began to be appreciated again in the late 1930s, and Wright made a triumphal visit to the Architectural Association in 1951. For the Trinity College design, however, Louis Kahn is a closer source, and Koralek had seen the Alfred Newton Richards Medical Research Building at the University of Pennsylvania, the first and most important phase of which had been completed in May 1960. A reference in the winning design is the use of trabeation in the exposed concrete floor slabs; as built, the relationship of concrete and stone is much closer to Kahn's work, particularly in the open corners of the respective buildings at ground-floor level. Richard Burton recalls being particularly impressed by the simple formality and symmetricality of Kahn's Bath House at Trenton, New Jersey, built in 1955. But more significantly, ABK developed as their own style the sense of weight and mass achieved by Kahn, and implanted it into sensitive settings of supreme historic renown.

1.49

The same simple strength found at Trinity can be clearly seen in the house designed in 1969 at the invitation of Dr Ernst Nebenzahl, State Controller of Israel, in the heart of Old Jerusalem. The same massing is evident, with the top floor of the long, simple main range projecting over cutaway corners, and similarly pierced fenestration through thick walls that forms an abstract rhythm across the sheer facades. But the setting is an intense one, overlooking the Western Wall, the Temple Mount and Dome of the Rock, and the materials are stone, thanks to an edict retained from the British mandate that requires all building in Old Jerusalem to be of stone. These very different locations confirmed ABK's reputation for designing buildings that are entirely modern, yet which respond to sensitive settings by their use of materials and forms. This contextualism was "a major strand in our work", says Koralek. "Finding ways of not resorting to pastiche but of relating in a positive way to historic locations was very important to us." It can

Berkeley Library: courtyard

1.49
The relationship between public and private at the British Embassy in Moscow is as complex as the political sensitivities of its construction.

1.50
In this County Council Headquarters at Offaly, Ireland, facades combine the transparency of glass with the warmth of timber screening.

1.51
For the County Council Headquarters at Tipperary, Ireland, the different functions of the building are articulated in its forms.

often involved visiting Gothic cathedrals, and Ahrends had had a magical introduction to Gothic by approaching Venice from the sea. Together the three of them produced a measured drawing of part of Salisbury Cathedral, a project which they brought to a successful conclusion despite access to a tower being barred by a verger who announced that permission would have to be sought from the Dean and Chapter. "The Dean's ill", he stated, and when asked if they could see the Chapter instead revealed that "the Chapter is a body". Their knowledge of the Trollopean minutiae of the Church of England hierarchy has never matched their fascination for its architecture.

Gothic became an important link in the chain of the young architects' evolving perceptions. For Ahrends it was clearly an emotional experience which he began to rationalise in terms Ruskin would have understood. It was, he explains, moving in both senses of the word: it could affect the emotions and its incompleteness, which was for Ruskin one of its main attributes, lent it dynamism and open-endedness, and invited movement through it. Echoing Ruskin's *Lamp of Obedience*, Ahrends saw Gothic as a necessary frame for expression. Koralek also saw Romanticism in Gothic and it segued into a growing interest in ornament. He was "struck by [Louis] Sullivan's writings", eagerly absorbing a book of Sullivan's drawings in the AA library. His readings of Sullivan suggested that "function was not just about usefulness, but also essence and

be well seen in their schemes of the 1960s and early 1970s: at Trinity, at Chichester Theological College, with their scheme for rebuilding St Anne's Soho, and at the Catholic chaplaincy and Keble College in Oxford. Had their proposals for the Post Office at St Martin's le Grand and the National Gallery been built, its importance as

a continuing theme in their work would have been more evident, but Koralek points to the firm's dental hospital in Dublin (c. 1995) as evidence of this continuing preoccupation. The Dover Heritage Centre designed in 1988 is another case of a building making a bold, sympathetic statement in a historic setting.

Meanwhile, the firm had established itself

in England. When Koralek headed for the United States, Burton had taken his place at Powell and Moya, and detailed the nurses' housing at Princess Margaret Hospital, Swindon, the first large-scale hospital built for the nationalised health service. He was then invited to be job architect for Powell and Moya's additions to Brasenose College

Berkeley Library: concrete shuttering

Berkeley Library: corner detail

Nebenzahl house, Jerusalem: context

Nebenzahl house, Jerusalem

nature", and form could have significance and meaning. Interspersed with the drawings, Koralek remembers, were occasional pages with just a small seed and an injunction, "remember the seed germ". Nature and organic growth could contribute to architecture and, by reversal, architecture was never a finite process.

Nature, Gothic and Sullivan were guides to an appreciation of form and meaning which led towards an interest in decoration. Gothic in particular, especially as interpreted

through Viollet-le-Duc (much promoted by John Summerson who lectured on history), showed how decoration and rational construction might be related. Pursuing similar themes led Burton to write a dissertation about Byzantine and Islamic architecture, and to propose the subversive idea that the Blue Mosque outshone the Hagia Sophia, for which his marker, an exponent of the Hagia Sophia, severely criticised him. Eventually, armed with several scholarships and the experience of foreign

travel during summer vacations, they decided to visit Persia to study Islamic architecture directly. Despite coinciding with the Suez crisis of 1956 – which provoked Burton's father and the actor Robert Donat, father of John who accompanied them, to send hundreds of telegrams begging their return – they studied how decoration and structure could be highly integrated, and the interaction of activities in the souk. The agglomeration of private spaces around a sinuous route, brought to life by

(BNC), planned in 1956 but only built with remodelled elevations in 1958–60. The slender infill range, mostly one room deep but with two staircases, spawned Powell and Moya's own brilliant career as designers of additions to Oxford and Cambridge colleges. At the moment when work was beginning on St Catherine's College, with Arne Jacobsen as its controversial choice of architect, Brasenose showed that British architects could also produce a modern yet sensitive design that extended right through from careful external finishes to the furniture. Much of the furniture was designed by Burton, with Peter Ahrends, who was then working as job architect on flats in Vauxhall Bridge Road for Julian Keable after a period with his father's practice in South Africa. The BNC block contrives to squeeze naturally into the heart of Oxford's historic townscape with elegant dignity, yet with no compromise of styles. While the fragmented geometry of its stepped lead roofs and penthouses became an unmistakable Powell and Moya trait, the

human activity, was another impression which Ahrends remembers. If the unsuccessful competition entry for rebuilding the Beirut souks is the most obvious result of this experience, the prevalence of complex, winding routes through many of their schemes shows the depth of this impression and the sensibilities with which they transformed it.

In parallel with the interest in decoration, there developed an interest in art. Both sprang in part from the realisation that architecture's expressive potential could be greatly enriched by adding visual richness, either mediated through the discipline of an integration between structure and decoration, or the equally demanding but very different process of working with other creative artists. It was perhaps from Burton, whose mother was a writer on art and and who had had the most overtly "artistic" education which continued into his studies with Coldstream, that this interest emanated most strongly. It is certainly in projects for which he took most responsibility, St Mary's Hospital, the British Embassy and his own house, that this comes across most strongly.

These were not fashionable ideas in the early 1950s, and in particular went against the Corbusier-fetish that many students in the year above them shared with tutors like Killick who taught them in the third year. Late Corbusier posed a difficult challenge for Killick, and especially his contemporary James Stirling. They found his departure from the five points of architecture which he

use of a broken structural grid infilled on different planes with a variety of materials was developed in a crisper, more dynamic fashion by ABK in subsequent commissions for higher education buildings. Two important commissions were passed to the fledgling firm by Powell and Moya, who after the success of BNC were offered more

work than they were prepared to handle.

The first of these was for a theological college in Chichester, where Philip Powell's father was a Canon of the cathedral. The brief was for 35 study-bedrooms, three staff flats, a library and a lecture room, which Burton and Ahrends set in four small blocks around a courtyard, bridged at first-floor level over

covered ways leading from the adjoining chapel to the main college buildings to the rear on Westgate. The route through a building is always emphasised by Ahrends, and it is key to understanding the planning of this complex building. Nicholas Taylor, writing in the *Architectural Review* for August 1965 (p. 90), commented on the affinities with

I was delighted when Richard Burton of ABK asked me if I would like to design the forecourt of the new British Embassy in Moscow, and had little notion of the problems there could be in such a complicated endeavour. Russia's climate alone presents great difficulties for any external works. There are such extremes of temperature (it would probably be under snow for five months of the year) that much paving in Russia hits the dust, so to speak, sooner or later.

Nevertheless, from my perspective it would be impossible to imagine that this project could have gone more smoothly. There was not one single hitch. My brief was very clear: to design a forecourt for the Embassy that would complement and enhance the building, and to provide an entrance that would be appropriate to its function as the main entrance. The materials were granite setts. However, in order to create some tonal and

textural contrast I proposed using "channels" together with the setts.

Artists and architects often seem to speak in very different languages, but we had none of those difficulties. Much was understood without the need for endless explanation.

The building is a lovely place to live and work, the scale is so well conceived, and the site, overlooking the river in the astonishing and mysterious city of Moscow, is perfect.

Tess Jaray

2.1
Context. The stairwell at Berkeley Library in Dublin incorporates a stained glass window.

2.2
Berkeley Library occupies a highly sensitive position at the centre of the Trinity College Dublin campus.

British Embassy, Moscow: public art installation by Tess Jaray

enunciated in the 1920s an abandonment of the very precepts of avant-garde modernism on which they were trying to establish a supposedly rational theory. Along with his colleague Bill Howell, Killick was working on the Roehampton estate where they "corrected" the aberrations of Corb's Unité d'Habitation; Stirling's Richmond flats performed the same exercise on the Maisons Jaoul. In what started to be a typical pattern, Ahrends, Burton and Koralek visited Ronchamp in November 1955, and were

overwhelmed by its light, surface, solid and void, rather than any relationship to the five points.

Romanticism was a reaction to the rationalism which the trio's immediate seniors sought in Le Corbusier. One of them, Tony Sheppard, remembers lifting the lecture podium, with Le Corbusier on it, onto a car which was wheeled around Bedford Square; Neave Brown persuaded the great man to produce a series of drawings over a meal in a restaurant. Arthur Korn's reaction to a

contemporary's project – "I hate zis thing" – licensed an emotional response in contrast to the propensity for demanding an explanation to every design decision. In this context, Ahrends, Burton and Koralek began to look at Frank Lloyd Wright, an interest which emerged in the second year, under tutors from ACP but principally Kenneth Capon and Tony Cox. Wright was unquestionably a "pioneer" of modern architecture – and visited the AA while they were students – but his intricate compositions, natural materials

2.2

BNC: "An acute understanding of infilling a slow-growth medieval city, a sympathetic massing of materials and skyline, and a subtle connection to existing pedestrian routes and communal activities." The broken massing is developed in a more complex, three-dimensional form than at Brasenose. As striking are the differences: the use of

brick and raw concrete, complete with Corbusian water spouts, and the love of angled surfaces and toplighting that were to be the two most repeated features of ABK's early work. "Skylit Seminary" was the headline in the *Architects' Journal* (18 August 1965, p. 387). The phrase referred specifically to the toplighting over the built-in alcove desk

provided for each study-bedroom and which give the facades their faceted rhythm, but it is a reminder of how important a role strong, directed light sources play in all early ABK schemes. Gillett House was a youthful piece of Brutalism that relates to the medieval buildings to its rear rather than to the adjoining playing fields to the south; now

Chichester Theological College

Chichester Theological College: context

Chichester Theological College: exterior

Chichester Theological College: detail

2.3
Flanked by the newer Arts Building, the Berkeley Library continues the college tradition of framing a succession of courts and gardens.

2.4
In front of the Old Library by Thomas Burgh, a forecourt is created on a podium, beneath which thousands of books are stored.

and complex forms did not follow the conventional enthusiasms of British architectural students. Rather as their different backgrounds set up a creatively critical relationship with modernism, so their mild rebellion against AA conventions demonstrated their growing confidence in attempting originality.

Enthusiasm for Wright also carried a price. It earned them the term "the country boys", and more seriously, might have underpinned the rural bias of their projects. In their last

year Ahrends submitted a forestry community in the highlands of Scotland, and Koralek an agricultural college. These settings were not unique; at the same time Cullinan offered an open prison. Reflecting on this, Ahrends recalls that he was looking for the "roughness and toughness of land, similar to South Africa" rather than an overt rejection of the city, but this does coincide with a time when British architects in general lacked any meaningful way of engaging with existing urban fabrics. Burton bucked the

trend with a music centre, another enduring interest, but situated near the Serpentine in Hyde Park, it avoided having to deal directly with infrastructure and buildings around.

Ironically, ABK's first two major projects, the Trinity College Dublin Library and Chichester Theological College, both demanded engagement with historic contexts and set a precedent which became a hallmark of the practice. Meeting these challenges evinced a further creative interpretation of another aspect of the AA's

these have been opened up, the setting has entirely changed.

Very different was the second job secured through the Powell and Moya connection. At Brasenose, Burton had established an extraordinarily good rapport with the client, corresponding on first-name terms with the bursar, Norman Leyland, at a time when Oxbridge etiquette was still extremely formal. When Leyland became director of the newly-founded Oxford Centre for Management Studies in 1965, Powell and Moya recommended ABK for its greenfield site close to the noisy ring road. The Centre is a college for grown-ups, with all the lectures, study and social facilities expected of an Oxford college but for middle managers on courses lasting up to six months. The study-bedrooms were thus designed to exacting standards, with split-level living and sleeping areas, and with a central, open library leading directly off the reception area so that the managers could not avoid walking through it. The main areas of the building are designed on a "tartan"

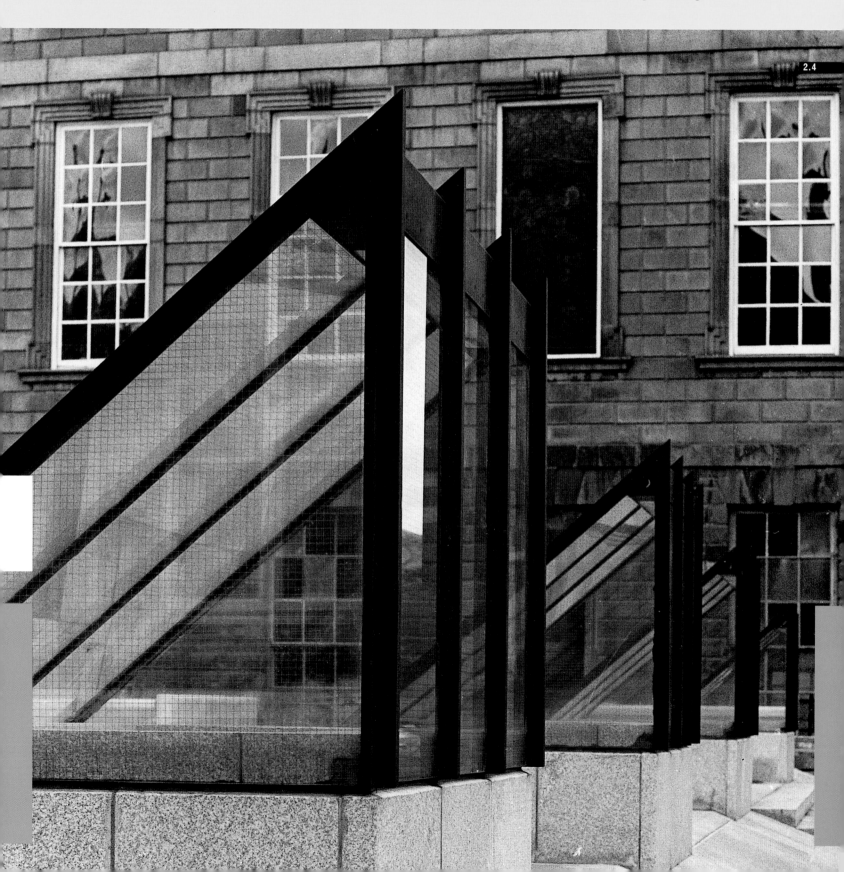

2.4

grid, where each unit square has four columns, so that at a typical internal junction there are four columns, allowing for services and partitions through the middle. Business science was then a new subject, and remains a fast-changing one, so the college was designed to be as flexible as possible. The building manager takes a rare delight in removing and rebuilding partition walls as required, while the library's size was doubled using the same system in 1985–86.

Templeton College has been ABK's longest running project: first commissioned in 1965, they last worked here in 1998, during which time the practice has been responsible for seven phases of development that hug the contours, creating a series of open courtyards protected from the worst of the traffic noise. The study-bedrooms take the ABK love of angles to an extra stage, with sheer sloping walls of glass – a feature exploited more fully in later phases and which served as a prototype for the accommodation subsequently added to

2.5

teaching. Burton suggests that Arthur Korn's lectures on urbanism (the basis of his book *History Builds the Town*) gave them the equipment to develop sensibilities towards urban development, though building in historic contexts was not Korn's main interest. From a loosely Marxist standpoint, Korn analysed urban development as an organic process, depending on economic and social forces rather than the interventions of leaders or architects. This message fitted into the interests of Ahrends, Burton and Koralek. It allowed them to place function and human activity, rather than formal or material preferences, at the centre of their design process, perhaps, following Ahrends' point, seeing their work as part of an ongoing flux.

Interestingly Koralek recalls that the main strength of the design he submitted for the Trinity Library competition was its plan, rather than its elevations. They showed traces of influence from Marcel Breuer, in whose office he was working, and from where he produced numerous competition entries in his own time. None of them satisfied him – not even Trinity, though after failing to send in earlier ones he determined to submit it come what may, partly to show he was contributing something to the practice which Ahrends and Burton were trying to establish in London. On winning the competition he returned to London where the practice formally opened. While he was concerned with the library's design development they were commissioned for the

Keble College, which has similar cross-ventilation. Most powerful of all, however, is the entrance facade, a patchwork of square planes in glass and, mainly, low-maintenance zinc, a lighter and more sophisticated rendition of the Brasenose aesthetic stretched to embrace a hillside. A stream on the site determined not only the angle of the

later phases but also the series of small pools that wind through the site, culminating in a narrow rill that cuts through the shallow steps that form such a dignified, considered entrance to the building, forcing the busy middle manager to slow down, look around and take stock. This was one of ABK's many collaborations with the landscape architect

James Hope, whose work has become an integral part of their larger projects and which was such an outstanding feature of Cummins Engines, and St Mary's Hospital, Newport, in particular.

The extension made to Keble College in two stages, in 1971–73 and 1975–78, under the supervision of Peter Ahrends, remains

2.5
The granite and white concrete facades of the Library represent the 20th century – in contrast to the 19th-century Museum by Deane and Woodward.

2.6
An aerial view of the college campus shows how well the Library and Arts Buildings match the rhythm of the existing spaces.

2.7
Berkeley Library is in fact an extension to the original library, designed by Thomas Burgh and built in 1732. It is the home of the Book of Kells.

2.8
The effect of the structure is to create a powerful trinity of architecture from the 18th, 19th and 20th centuries, framing the forecourt.

Chichester Theological College, which consequently fell in large part to Ahrends and Burton.

With its brick walls, timber windows and concrete trimmings, Chichester shows some affinities with the "Brutalist" work of the time, notably their former tutors Killick and Smithson, or Stirling and Gowan's Ham Common flats. Brutalism's chronicler Reyner Banham suggested its practitioners sought to create "une architecture autre", which made no reference to tradition and developed

purely from commonly available materials. To some extent the college might be seen in this light, but Banham continued to define Brutalism in largely formal and material terms. To apply these further at Chichester is seriously misleading, for its design develops much more from context and use than the way brick meets concrete. The placing of the building, remembers Ahrends, came from recognising the importance of the route between the house which already housed part of the college, and the church its

members used as a chapel. Creating its own courtyard and treating the new library as an internal court, their building became a sequence of events on the route. By analogy, the individual study-bedrooms, though small and plainly finished, have numerous different characteristics which suggest separate tasks. An opening window lights the main body of the space and has a window seat to suggest sociability, while a roof light illuminates the recessed desk. Like even the smallest aspect of

the best-known of the firm's early English work and perhaps the boldest of its interventions in a historic setting. William Butterfield's most spectacular secular work, Keble was just beginning to be appreciated as a masterpiece of Victorian Brutalism in the late 1960s, and to produce a neighbour that was neither compromising nor compromised

was a unique challenge. Following an invited interview, ABK were appointed in 1969 to extend Keble's accommodation on an adjoining site recommended in a development plan by Casson and Conder a year earlier. Whereas most public commissions require a building to attract users from outside, an Oxford college remains enclosed

and self-contained. Ahrends suggested that the existing nineteenth-century houses could be retained and linked by a covered way, but the college had determined on a new building and had begun fundraising. This concept, however, survives in the sunken, glazed walkway that forms the lowest layer of the inner glass skirt that ripples round the

2.9
Revised proposal for the National Gallery extension, amended in response to criticisms after ABK had already 'won' the competition.

2.10
The tower did not form part of the original scheme, but was added in response to a revised brief. The scheme was refused planning permission.

2.9

theology, the smallest rooms in the college defy single interpretations.

Just as it is impossible to extrapolate the development of ABK or Ahrends, Burton and Koralek as individuals from their experiences at the AA, so it is ridiculous to suggest that the practice's first 40 years directly unfolded from Chichester and the Trinity Library. But those projects introduced features which

became hallmarks: an interest in complex compositions which resolve into spaces of varied character; movement into and through a building and its precinct, which brings the rich complexity to life, and by extension an appreciation of context but which never becomes literal. At root, their work is about experience. It demands movement at least and possibly habitation,

whether through the subterranean path at Keble, or to appreciate the composition of the British Embassy in Moscow. The interior spaces, whether the rooms at Chichester, the housing at Basildon or Burton's own house, have a complexity which enriches use, not for its own sake. Above all, they never pose final static answers; rather they open more opportunities.

inner quadrangle of the replacement of the building and roots it so firmly to the ground. The angled brick plinth so frequently seen in ABK's buildings of the 1970s here forms an embankment to the inner grassed quadrangle. There is an acute sense of being in a cloister, where the members of the college collectively experience at close

quarters the materials that form its "sheltering skin", or what Ahrends terms "materiality and movement". He speaks of a "site with a hard edge to it", constrained as Keble was by surrounding streets, and that the solution with its external stair towers respects Kahn's notion of served and servant spaces. The scheme has been likened to a

snail, with a hard honey brick shell to the street, and a soft glazed underbelly within, that unwinds from a five-storey spiral staircase and steps sequentially to one hard by Butterfield's hall – or did before the lowest section was cruelly lopped off in 2001 in favour of a new building. It is the first use of a curve in ABK's built work, later to become

Keble College, Oxford: brick facade

Keble College, Oxford: quad

Keble College, Oxford: glass walkway

Keble College, Oxford: glass facade

2.10

One dramatic sketch of the unbuilt Mary Rose Museum captures this essence. A horizontal line makes an armature but two curves peel away from it; a third mirrors one about a lesser axis. There is an underlying structure, but it is open to change, to shift and fluctuation which might overwhelm it without leading to definite locations. Instead – this can be quite literal – they might suggest the

complex tides of the Solent which caused the ship to flounder, themselves a metaphor for the incalculable fluctuations of modernity against which architecture can offer temporary, though effective, solace.

In the final analysis it is this capacity for their architecture to be a portal rather than a terminus that sets them apart from other British architects. Architecture enables other

opportunities; it is not an end in itself. Not for them the obsession with proportional systems or reducing the width of housing units to 10 and a half feet; ironically the most inventive originators of architectural forms in their generation are Realists rather than Formalists, and their work unfolds as narrative rather than announcing itself through rhetorical gestures.

one of their hallmarks, and Ahrends suggests that its sense of movement represents the order and direction of the building towards its neighbour – intended ways through the end of the adjoining range were not developed as first planned. ABK's honey-coloured brick and angled dark glass are, moreover, a sophisticatedly simple contrast to Butterfield's work. The treatment here is comparable with the Trinity College library in countering mass with mass: there is no strongly expressed grid or box-like forms that, following Brasenose, became a stock solution to building new accommodation at Oxford or Cambridge. Moreover, while the materials and bold forms are hard, the curves encourage an organic imagery new in ABK's work. The mixture of hard yet soft is perhaps an underlying secret of the building's success. Ahrends claims to have discovered Albi Cathedral, with its massive medieval brick buttressing, only some 30 years later, though it was a familiar motif to Butterfield thanks to its publication in *The Ecclesiologist*

2.11
The facade of the Dover Heritage Centre addresses the existing building which adjoins it.

2.12
A glazed structure forms a crescent-shaped curve, framing the archeological remains of the 'Classis Britannica' and 'Saxon Shore' forts.

2.13
The combination of grey and cream brick in the Heritage Centre responds to other buildings in the area, including Dover Castle itself.

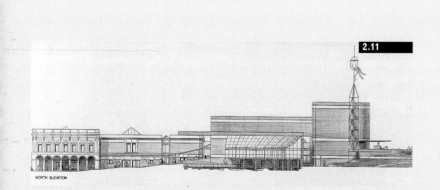

2.12

2.11

NORTH ELEVATION

1 Much later, during the practice's darkest hour under onslaught from Prince Charles, another echo would resound. Klaus Hinrichsen, an art historian living in Highgate, contacted Ahrends to ask if he were related to Bruno Ahrends. He had fond memories of Ahrends *grandpère* organising what amounted to a university in an internment camp. Perhaps one display of British philistinism provoked memories of another. In any case, it provided evidence that the wonderfully cosmopolitan, cultivated and assimilated Jewish culture of Mitteleuropa had survived its worst moment and was alive in north London.

2.13

in 1847; it is nevertheless curious how affinities can be drawn across centuries of western culture.

ABK had earlier produced a smaller piece of contextual infill for central Oxford. This is an addition tucked behind the Old Palace, a house of 1622–28 on St Aldate's that became the University's Roman Catholic Chaplaincy in 1896 and was refronted by Russell Cox in c.1955. Ahrends' work was commissioned in 1965 by Father Michael Hollings, a progressive leader in the Liturgical Movement that swept through Roman Catholicism in the mid–1960s. Completed to a revised design in 1972, as at Keble ABK countered a prestigious neighbour by a building that is different but equal. Their building respects the proportions of the Old Palace – long horizontal bands of glazing are equally possible in timber or concrete framed construction – but ABK's range is quite different in its stepped facade and use of the blond brick that characterises Keble and subsequent projects. Whitmore Court,

2.14

2.14

The project for St Anne's Church, Soho, incorporates the 1802 bell tower which was all that remained of the church after the Second World War.

2.15

Undertaken in 1964, the scene for the restoration project was an unloved and poverty-stricken urban zone, vastly different from today's Soho.

2.15

Basildon (1973–75) is a mixed development of flats for single young people and the elderly where this stepped profile and honey brick can also be seen. There is residential accommodation at the chaplaincy too, for eight study-bedrooms with a shared kitchen and roof terrace occupy the top floors, set over a library, meeting rooms, and weekday chapel, all served by a broad entrance hall with built-in seating that is a comfortable place to be while encouraging exploration through the building. The main chapel is a dual-purpose space that serves as a hall for meetings – and examinations – during the week. With so much accommodation piled on to such a tiny site, it is striking how the principal spaces are still largely top-lit; such directed light gives the entrance meeting area its individuality and the worship spaces their spirituality. Here, too, is one of the first examples of the angled brick plinth between the straight line of the pavement and the irregular one of the building which became a signature of ABK's work through the 1970s.

Chaplaincy, Oxford: exterior

Chaplaincy, Oxford: chapel

The early 1970s saw ABK expand their repertoire with a series of smaller public commissions that took the particularities of their style away from historic cities into new and growing towns, and into suburbia. They also mark a move away from building entirely in brick and concrete towards the use of steel. Burton suggests that an impetus for

this was their commission in March 1966 to build a new public library in Redcar: it was a steel town and the local authority insisted upon the local material as being most appropriate. In fact, the first phase of ABK's one school in England, in the overgrown village of Thurmaston, Leicestershire, was built of steel as early as 1966–68.

At the time, Leicestershire was the most enterprising education authority in Britain, thanks to its director Stewart Mason. Leicestershire brought the concept of open planning to secondary education, so that it is easy to overlook its early experiments for primary children, and ABK's Eastfield School, Thurmaston, was almost

2.16
Underground car-parking was a feature of the St Anne's Church design, with the lightweight glass and mesh structure supported by a concrete base.

2.17
A glass and steel lattice configuration was also proposed for the Post Office Headquarters building in London.

2.18
The external steel structure housed blinds for solar control. Situated within view of St Paul's Cathedral, a maximum height of 30m was stipulated.

2.18

2.17

contemporary with the Ministry of Education's own prototype, Eveline Lowe School, Southwark. Eastfield is clever because the pairs of classrooms have common cloakrooms and activities areas, but are sufficiently separated to be easy to supervise. Changes in level also encourage separation and further ease supervision.

Steps lead down from the entrance to an open hall, set under a stepped glazed roof that is again an ABK trademark. It is tempting to link this roof profile, often associated with parallelepiped spaces, with Koralek's work, for it appears in his Arts Faculty building at Trinity College, Dublin (1969–80), over the library that he brought to

fruition for Portsmouth Polytechnic (now University, 1972–77) and over the atrium at his branch of John Lewis, Kingston (1979–90). Yet what distinguishes the work of the 1970s is that features initially characteristic of one partner become increasingly homogeneous as the range of buildings and variety of materials increases. The game of

Thurmaston School: assembly hall

Thurmaston School: assembly hall

Thurmaston School: circulation route

2.19

2.19
Set in a beautiful garden site, study bedrooms at Chichester Theological College required careful planning to maintain routes to and from the chapel.

2.20
Detailing of the exterior of John Lewis in Kingston involved smaller elements whose scale relates well to the river and surrounding buildings.

2.21
Moreover, the brief for the Kingston department store included provision for a main road to pierce through the heart of the building.

determining "who did what", so tempting yet so inapposite because of the continuous intellectual debate between the three partners, becomes more difficult as the involvement of later partners and assistants also has to be considered. The symmetrical, patent glazing and higher, stepped centre-piece found in the classroom facades were to become a regular feature of work by all the partners, yet these features are most often compared with Stirling and Gowan's Engineering Building less than five miles away.

ABK's formative building was a prestigious copyright library. The pair of libraries for which they were commissioned in the late 1960s were on very different scales. In 1959 the Roberts Report recommended that towns with populations of under 40,000 should lose their status as independent library authorities. Redcar and Maidenhead, both smaller but targeted for regional expansion and growing fast, objected. Eventually, both secured funding for new buildings, whose

Portsmouth Polytechnic

Trinity College Arts Building

2.20

2.21

briefs were developed with the Department of Education and Science as an initiative to make libraries more welcoming to the user. Redcar's came first, built in 1968–71 on a site adjacent to a former school that was being adapted as a community centre. ABK created a cultural centre on the edge of the shopping area, reached by a new pedestrian route.

Glazing an existing cloister to form a winter garden linked the old and new buildings, while a coffee bar was a further enticement for potential readers. Inside, the building's steel frame is strongly expressed and the hexagonal holes of its castellated beams treated as a decorative motif – a theme that was repeated in the firm's

subsequent industrial work. Maidenhead (1970–73) is larger and the division of light and heavy materials more awkward. Its space frame roof, which is supported on eight concrete piers and was built first, appears to float over the building's solid red brick and concrete core. The chamfered plinth of red paviours from which it rises thus takes on a

2.22

2.22
An extension to the Whitworth Art Gallery in Manchester places a new gallery space in an old courtyard behind the existing building.

greater significance in weighting the building to the ground and separating it from the dross of its surroundings. Inside, the continuous glazing at upper level gives an even light across the building.

In 1972 ABK was invited to produce a development plan for the then Portsmouth Polytechnic's Ravelin House site near the city centre, and Ahrends prepared a detailed plan for the triangular site. Because of financial cutbacks, only the library was built, under Koralek's supervision. Had the library scheme been completed to the original design, its stepped plan and section would have been comparable to those at the Arts Faculty at Trinity College, Dublin. Instead there is a single wedge of a ziggurat that is a cascading roof of glass over a coffered concrete construction. It is unusual to find a deep plan, security-conscious library choosing natural ventilation over air conditioning, and it is an early example of architects working with an impecunious client to achieve a low-cost, green scheme

Maidenhead Library: interior

Maidenhead Library: exterior

Maidenhead Library: truss roof

2.25

2.23
The Roman Catholic
Chaplaincy in Oxford (1972) is
an extension to the 17th-century
Bishop's Palace. The stepped
facade echoes its gables.

2.24
The new building connects to
the old Bishop's Palace on three
levels, so that the old building is
fully integrated into the new
complex.

2.25
The new entrance to Trinity
College forms a circulation
spine from Nassau Street
through the heart of the Arts
Building to the campus beyond.

for a large building. The quality suffered by having to be left uncompleted, although in 1986–90 the practice returned to make a small addition for special collections that gave a curved form to the elevation previously left bare.

Issues of low cost and sustainability also inform the housing built by the firm for Basildon New Town Development Corporation. ABK had built only one scheme of housing in the 1960s, and this was for a private housing association formed in 1966 by five university academics and their families. A line of five linked houses was built in 1968–69 on a hilltop site outside Headington village, designed to present a strong image to the road while ensuring unusual privacy behind a double skin of walls that shelter a common forecourt between the public road and private forecourt. The form of the houses is not unlike that of the formula adopted at Brasenose, with piers of solid forticrete walling contrasted with full-height panels of lightweight cladding and aluminium

Portsmouth Polytechnic

Portsmouth Polytechnic at night

Redcar Library

Portsmouth Polytechnic

2.26

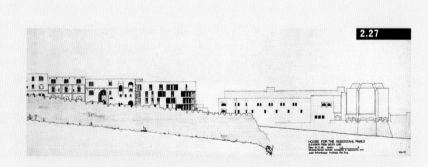
2.27

2.28

2.26
The Old City of Jerusalem is visible from Mount Zion, and the Mount of Olives. Its strong religious associations were a key consideration.

2.27
The Nebenzahl house continues an existing line of buildings inside the old City Wall.

2.28
The building's deep window openings are angled to filter light and reveal the many different views that the site commands.

2.29
All external surfaces are made from stone, but detailing is reminiscent of other ABK designs in concrete.

2.29

2.30
The residential building for
Keble College, Oxford, creates a
dialogue with William
Butterfield's imposing Victorian
structure.

windows. Seen in a stepped line along the road, there is an interweaving of heights and angles, the picturesque room shapes made possible by the spine wall that runs back the length of each house and giving a sense of movement to the terrace. The fluid rhythm of interconnecting planes is similar to the more curvaceous plan of Howell Killick

Partridge and Amis' Houses for Visiting Mathematicians, built at Warwick University a year later.

The Basildon housing was to be far less muscular, but similarly to use traditional load-bearing construction, in this case brick. Basildon's image is not an appealing one, even among the New Towns designated after

the war and now so unfashionable. Yet in terms of architectural and social activity it is unfairly derided, for in 1963 its target population was revised upwards to 106,000 (it is still growing), and a second, more interesting range of housing gave greater variety to the townscape than is found, for example, at Stevenage and Harlow. ABK

Public housing, Northlands

Public housing, Chalvedon

Public housing, Chalvedon

Public housing, Northlands

2.31

The height of the outer wall of the new Keble building steps progressively down, to allow Butterfield's hall to be seen from the road.

2.32

Inside the inner courtyard, the glass planes of the Keble building continue to respect the powerful presence of the older buildings nearby.

were commissioned in 1968 to design housing at Chalvedon, immediately adjacent to the first areas of the New Town developed with conventional semis in the early 1950s. The contrast is striking. Chalvedon is built at relatively high density, but with a high proportion of single-storey patio housing, with internal courtyards, developing the experiments made by Phippen, Randall and Parkes at The Ryde, Hatfield, in 1963–66. Deep-planned single-storey housing is equally suited to families, the elderly and the disabled. At Chalvedon the one- and two-storey ranges were set out in 1973–77 around broad squares, with separate areas for cars to the side, exploiting changing levels in the site. The units are built of brick, tile and stained timber, a reaction to the costs and problems then emerging from the use of non-traditional materials, and this and the overall layout are immediately reminiscent of low-rise elements of Ralph Erskine's Byker Estate, particularly of the Gordon area developed in 1974–76. Like Byker,

Chalvedon's later phases were informed by a programme of feedback from residents, and it was one of the first projects to develop the requirements of the Skeffington Report (1969) on public consultation to include a social psychologist, Peter Ellis, in the team. Following the success of Chalvedon, ABK were invited in 1974 to develop the

Northlands/Felmore area immediately to the north, where building started in 1977. Burton's design was a response not only to high-density planning issues but also to energy issues, combining an efficient district heating system with a careful layout, insulation, steep pitched roofs suitable for solar panels and deep eaves to control solar gain in

summer. The heating pipes are set over the covered walkways that run up the south-facing slope, and link the terraces – another feature reminiscent of later phases of Byker.

Opportunities for public sector work, increasingly constrained by inflation in the 1970s, were all but terminated by the 1979 election, save in specialised areas such as

2.33

2.33

Fellows' Square is a new space created by the construction of the Trinity College Arts Building, with an Alexander Calder 'stabile' on the lawn.

hospital and prison design. For ABK the greatest loss due to government cutbacks was the loss of a project for rebuilding the Post Office's headquarters in St Martin's le Grand by St Paul's Cathedral. It had been another challenge in a dense historic context. ABK had found a champion in Eric Bedford, Chief Architect to the Ministry of Works, and were interviewed for the British Library and National Theatre commissions in the mid–1960s before securing the GPO job. The scheme, for a progressive lattice-framed curtain-walled block with a bridge link from Paternoster Square through to ground level, was carefully developed on the latest *bürolandschaft* principles with both management and the unions, and was curtailed just as the designs were completed. Nevertheless it gave ABK valuable experience of designing large-scale offices.

ABK's first commercial buildings were on very different suburban sites entirely devoid of context. First, in 1972–74, came warehouses and a retail outlet for Habitat at

Post Office HQ, London: model

2.34
Cardiff Bay was once the largest coal shipping port in the world. In the mid-19th century Bailey's Heavy Engineering workshop repaired ships docked nearby.

2.35
ABK's design for an education centre retains the original cast and wrought iron structure, whose renovation extended to the huge transporter crane.

2.36
The Techniquest Science Centre includes new elements within the old shell, itself radically extended.

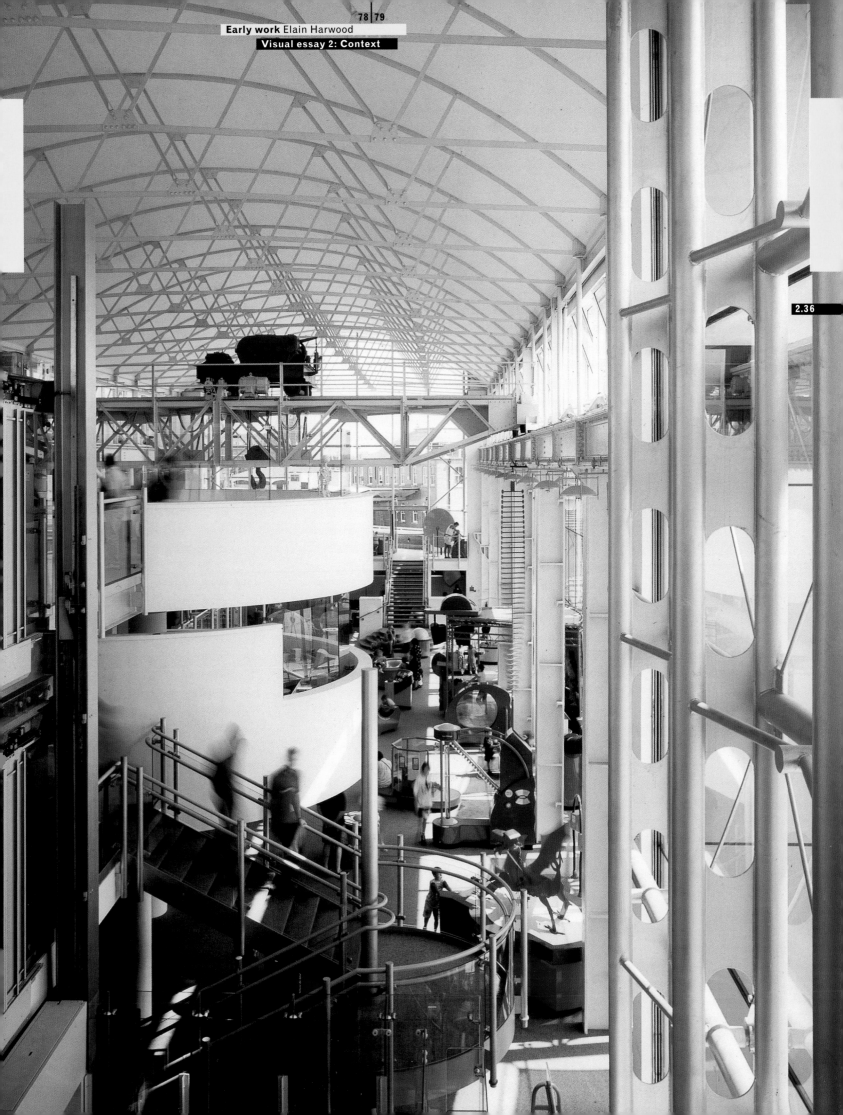

2.36

Wallingford, developed by Richard Burton with Terence Conran. It combined a warehouse, showroom and café, made of corrugated cement sheet on an ABK chamfered plinth and emblazoned with the Habitat logo like a gigantic low-loader. Habitat stimulated a fascination with industrial building that had lain dormant since ABK's student scheme for a colliery workshop, but which brought out all the firm's interest in daylighting, structure and space. But it was at Shotts, outside Motherwell, far from the Home Counties, that ABK were to build their most ambitious industrial project. Just before the GPO scheme had been cancelled, Kevin Roche called them, saying he had recommended ABK for additions to be made by the Cummins Engine Company to their plant there. Cummins had opened a factory in 1946, in a conventional saw-tooth building provided by the Scottish Development Agency that was at odds with the firm's enlightened policy of using good design as a

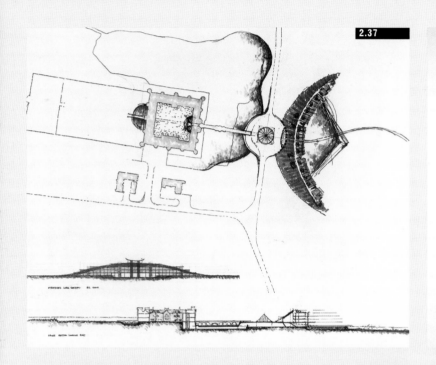

2.37

Sketch for a hotel and conference centre at Herstmonceaux Castle, with allusions to the visual language of the country house 'ha-ha'.

2.38

Seen from above, the existing castle at Herstmonceaux provides an imposing context for the proposed new building.

stimulus for its workers and its outside image. Ahrends proposed a complete redevelopment plan rather than make piecemeal additions, adapting the original building as offices and distribution centre, with a new factory behind. The design enabled production to be continued through the construction period, and included a

canteen, placed centrally so that the office and manufacturing workforces would have to meet, and where they could look down on the completed engines leaving the site. In the factory areas Ahrends provided large bays where workmen could eat their sandwiches in comfort, with large glazed windows angled inwards to avoid solar gain. An answering

angle for the corrugated steel walling above countered excessive machinery noise. The effect was to create a distinctive lozenge pattern to the side elevations. Walkways placed high over the factory floor linked to car parking on higher adjoining ground give the factory its other distinctive image, one of movement contrasted with the giant

2.41

2.39
At the Visitor Centre in Waterford, ABK make use of a blank white wall to shield passers-by from the bold glass facade of its new extension.

2.40
Inside Waterford Visitor Centre, the full volume of the interior space has been opened up, while using existing columns to support gallery spaces.

2.41
A restaurant extension to the Waterford Visitor Centre allows maximum light to enter, while retaining a subtle exterior and privacy for diners.

2.42

2.42
Overlooking the river and the
city of Moscow, the apartments
within the British Embassy are
designed to host parties for
large numbers of guests.

corrugated steel skirt draped across the factory floor. Again, there is a dynamic in the architecture created by the importance of the route, both for the workforce, and for the engines whose assembly moves through the building from back to front.

From the mid–1960s two strands of architecture emerged in England: the concept of the serviced space, celebrated by the Smithsons and exemplified in the principles of High-Tech, and building as a carefully considered solution to a specific

brief. The individuality of each of ABK's buildings stands as a contrast to most of the work produced in these years; it is rare to find such large commissions placed firmly in the second category. Many of these ideas coalesced in their first scheme for the ill-

Cummins Engines factory: walkways

Cummins Engines factory at night

2.43
In contrast to the bombastic monumentalism of its neighbours, the Embassy aims to present a more transparent aspect to the river.

fated National Gallery competition in 1982: the mass of the front office block with the columniation of its fenestration reminiscent of the Berkeley Library, and contrasted with the curve of galleries behind, whose daylighting was a development from ABK's

first venture into gallery design, made as early as 1963 for the Kasmin Gallery. The result was a surprisingly mobile solution to a complex brief that had to combine gallery space with lettable commercial offices, cut through by a route from Leicester Square

centred on a coffee shop. The early 1980s marked a momentous turning point in ABK's fortunes. The change in government and changes in architectural fashion came together for ABK in the debacle of the National Gallery competition, when their

2.43

hard-fought scheme was rejected in a reversal of the original brief, amidst acrimony from outsiders. It brought the firm unwanted public attention, in a very different climate to that which had heralded their exhibition at the RIBA Heinz Gallery in October 1980, when *Building Design* described a history of "fairy tale proportions" that had brought them to "one of the highest pinnacles of RIBA acclaim" (24 October 1980). It is that success, so rare and extraordinary, that this essay has sought to rediscover.

Kasmin Art Gallery, London

Kasmin Art Gallery, London

Kasmin Art Gallery, London

3.1

Light and space. A 1978 drawing of the fully glazed atrium space at the headquarters of Johnson and Johnson, long before atria were common.

3.1

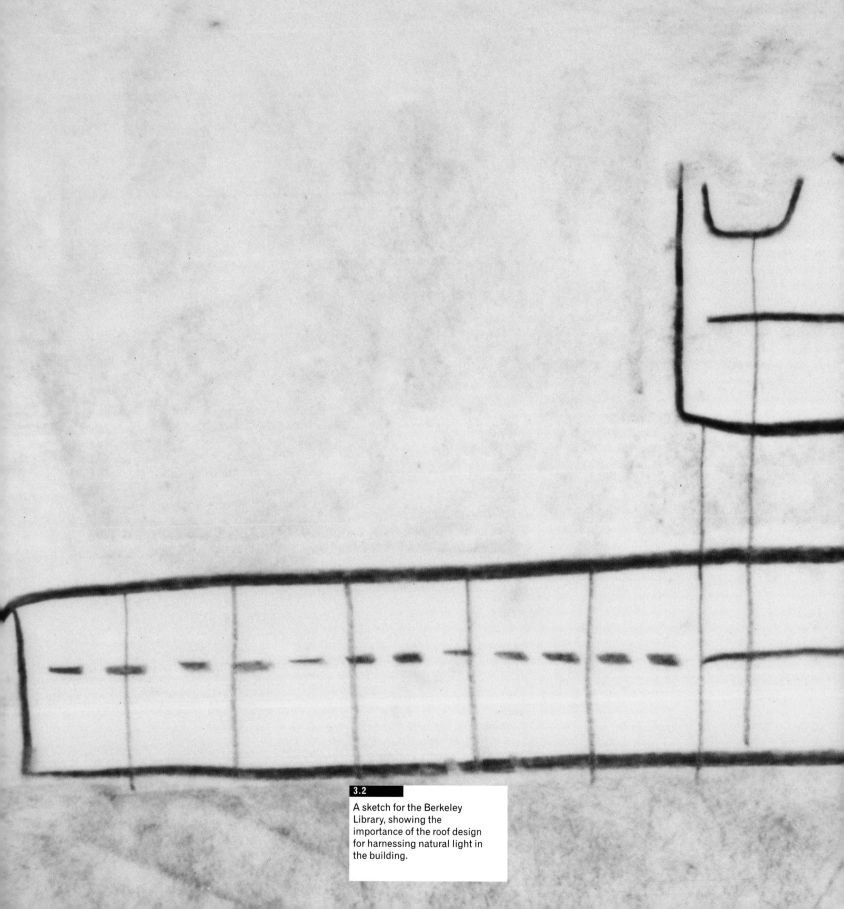

A sketch for the Berkeley Library, showing the importance of the roof design for harnessing natural light in the building.

3.2

3.3

The study spaces at Berkeley
Library are flooded with natural
light.

3.4

The top-lit reading room.

3.4

3.5

3.6

3.5

The glazed sloping roof at
Portsmouth Polytechnic's
library covers a large interior
volume, an open-plan reading
room bathed in natural light.

3.6

The three-storey roof is the
most dynamic element in the
building's design, both inside
and out.

3.9

3.8

3.7
The design for the Whitworth
Art Gallery ensures that the
space is well illuminated for the
display of sculpture.

3.8
In the library at Chichester
Theological College the top-lit
space contrasts with the study
bedrooms, which deploy a
mixture of top- and cross-light.

3.9
At Templeton College, the top-lit
library space forms the focus of
study, with teaching and
administrative areas arranged
around its perimeter.

3.10

The glass roof in John Lewis gives the store an extraordinary sense of openness. This view is from the Waitrose supermarket on the ground level.

3.11

Reflective louvres are used to provide careful control of light levels. The system has considerable environmental benefits for the building.

3.12

Completed in 1963, the art gallery for John Kasmin is an early ABK commission. The sculptural form of the section connects space to light source.

3.13

The reception space at WH Smith's headquarters takes the form of a top-lit drum. From here, the entire building is accessed by a diagonal route.

3.14

The proposed Opera House at Compton Verney uses glass and shutters to illuminate the night landscape until moments before a performance begins.

3.15

By day, with the shutters open, the glazed exterior of the auditorium allows spectacular views of the landscape and the Robert Adam house beyond.

3.16

Spaces for worship. The glass and steel exterior of St Anne's in Soho would have made it the most public sacred space in London – day or night.

3.17

The main hall at the Roman Catholic Chaplaincy in Oxford mixes top-lighting techniques reminiscent of Ronchamp, with recessed artificial roof lights.

3.18

The smaller chapel at the Oxford Chaplaincy is an intense, light-filled space .

3.19

At Chichester Theological College, the facade reflects the mixed use of top- and cross-lighting in each of the building's study-bedrooms.

3.20

Beside the traditional opening window, which offers views out over the landscape, a carefully articulated space is top-lit to allow for focused study.

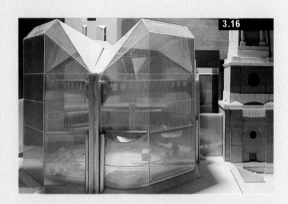

3.20

Ireland Frank McDonald

Dublin was a very different place in 1961 when Paul Koralek won a competition to design a new library for Trinity College. With the singular exception of Michael Scott's

Busaras (1952), the city had no modern buildings; its Georgian fabric was still intact, mainly because – as one visiting English critic observed later – "the Irish were too poor to pull it down". Trinity itself was an effete enclave of "West Brits" right in the middle of

the city, cut off from the mainstream of Irish life, thanks to a long-standing ban by John Charles McQuaid, the authoritarian Archbishop of Dublin, on Catholics attending the avowedly Protestant college. Indeed, a Union Jack run up to mark VE Day in 1945 had been burnt by nationalistic students from its main rival, University College Dublin.

The new library was to be Trinity's first building project for 30 years. As one of the few libraries entitled to receive a copy of every book published in Britain and Ireland, Trinity needed extra storage space to house more than 820,000 volumes, and reading rooms with an overall capacity of 469 were also required for a then much smaller student

population of 2,600. An appeal had been launched in 1958 to raise money for the project which, as J.V. Luce, the college's Professor of Classics and chairman of the fund-raising committee, said was not going to cost much more than the price of two modern fighter aircraft (the Irish Air Corps didn't even have one at the time). Among

3.21
The walkway skirting the ground floor of Keble College is protected by a glazed canopy. By day it has the quality of a conservatory.

3.22
At its northern end the covered walkway opens out into a social space, whose intimate meeting areas take advantage of the glazed wall for their lighting.

3.23
A similar effect is achieved in the circular cafe space at John Lewis, where side- and top-lighting create a dramatic social space.

We wanted a contemporary building, not pastiche, but something that would live in peace with the Butterfield elevations. Butterfield said he wanted his buildings to be "gay", but his brick follows you everywhere. Using glass in the inner wall of ABK's building gives marvellous reflections, and the colour of the brick they used picks up the pieces of stone – and there's actually quite a lot of it – in Butterfield's walls.
   This was the first time I had had anything to do with architecture. I was struck by the importance of the relationship between architect and client, and how high emotions can go. Some of my colleagues said, "if we do it that way I'll never go into that part of the college". We were all ambitious for a great building. We wanted something that would be noticed, a great piece of modern architecture, and it is one of the finest in Oxford of that period.

Professor Jim Griffin
Former White's Professor of Moral Philosophy, University of Oxford

those who responded generously were the Ford Foundation and the Guinness-funded Iveagh Trust. In what was clearly a move to lure the college out of its ivory tower, the Government agreed to pay half the capital cost, then estimated at £640,000. The only condition was that the Library in Trinity would co-operate with the National Library in providing practical help to Government departments and other public bodies.
   Incredibly, of the 218 entries in the design competition, only nineteen were from Ireland – indicating either a paucity of indigenous architectural talent or, more likely, a wariness among Irish architects to become involved in a high-profile project at Trinity. Though Michael Scott and Partners received honourable mention, all three prize-winning schemes and two more that were highly commended came from abroad.
   Paul Koralek was 28 at the time he designed the competition-winning entry, working from a "tiny" apartment on East 63rd Street in New York. He had never been to

3.24

It is a rare sight in factories, but at Cummins Engines in Scotland, workers can look out of the windows at the view. Lunch can be eaten sitting in the window bays.

Dublin and didn't visit the city in advance to see the proposed site. There were not many other points of reference either; according to him, only one new university library (Sheffield) had been built in Britain since the Second World War. Later, after winning the competition, Koralek recalls meeting Dublin Corporation's then chief planning officer, Michael O'Brien, who was a regular visitor to the Archbishop's palace in Drumcondra. "His only concern was whether the building could be seen from outside college and, somewhat disingenuously, we said 'no'. He said, 'Well, that's all I need to know' and that's how we got planning permission."

Yet the scheme was a radical intervention in the Oxbridge-like fabric of Trinity College. This issue had been raised by one of the assessors, Professor Franco Albini of the Istituto Universitario di Architettura in Venice; what worried him was that Koralek's design, though "carefully worked out", had not given "any indication that the problem of inserting the new architecture within the present surroundings has been faced up to". Given that the most recent addition was a 1930s neo-classical Reading Room, context was an issue. "Immediately one heard that a new building was to be inserted in Trinity, one had misgivings", said the *Irish Builder*. "It

3.24

would be out of place. It would ruin the whole atmosphere of the College. Gone forever would be that feeling of stepping into another century when passing through Trinity's gates." Though Albini abstained from voting for the winning entry, it didn't matter. The other assessors, notably Sir Hugh Casson and Raymond McGrath, principal architect of the Office of Public Works, believed that Koralek's "consciously modern" design showed "enough good taste and judgement to encourage confidence that, when built, the new library will be a notable addition to the architecture of the college".

And so, indeed, it was. As soon as the judges announced that his entry had won, Koralek teamed up with Richard Burton and Peter Ahrends to develop the design. The project became the first and probably the closest of their collaborations, and when the Library was completed in July 1967, it was immediately hailed as an architectural masterpiece. As the *Irish Builder* observed, "The new building fits into its eighteenth century surroundings ideally... Already it seems to have always been there. There is no feeling of awkwardness. It lies there quite at home and quite capable of comparing with its austere neighbours". Contrary to what Prof Albini believed, ABK had taken full

3.25

3.26
The play of natural light on brick at Keble College.

3.27
Fair-faced brick is washed by natural light from overhead in the stairwells at Keble.

3.28
The wards at St Mary's Hospital, Isle of Wight, are lit by daylight from overhead, in addition to the bedside window openings.

3.29
Hooke Park's bright open spaces come from windows along the apex of the curved roof space.

Berkeley Library, Dublin.

Berkeley Library, Dublin.

Berkeley Library, Dublin.

Berkeley Library, Dublin.

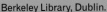

account of the context in designing their cutting-edge Brutalist pile. It was placed very specifically to create a new courtyard between Deane and Woodward's Museum, so beloved of Ruskin, and Thomas Burgh's 1732 Library, thereby providing a natural extension of the sequence of quadrangles that provide the backbone of the college's layout.

Edward McParland, the distinguished architectural historian and Trinity Fellow, has observed that the podium of the Berkeley Library – as it is officially known – is "the only carefully thought-out transition from one square to another in the entire college". And because it is elevated (over the book storage area below), it also creates a "sense of occasion" framed by fine buildings of the eighteenth and nineteenth centuries. Unlike the old Library, "it does not have a lucid classical plan. Instead, it is full of secluded cells picturesquely disposed, naturally lighted and conducive, it is hoped, to study", Dr McParland remarked in his book on the buildings of Trinity College. In its review, the *Irish Builder* commented on the "monastic-like formation of the great Iveagh Hall" – the Library's main reading space – and the Morrison room above. Harry Allberry, the magazine's editor, was particularly smitten

by the use of Douglas fir shuttering for the Library's white, self-finishing reinforced concrete. "So marked is the timber pattern that one expected to see the sap oozing from it!", he marvelled. He was also impressed by the Library's tall bay windows in curved glass, which are still the finest set of fenestration on any modern building in Dublin.

In a review verging on the ecstatic, Allberry remarked on the "complete harmony" of the grey-toned rubber floor covering and the pale gold, veneered Finnish plywood of the cabinets and shelving inside and how all of the furniture had been designed by the architect and manufactured in the joinery works of the main contractor, G&T Crampton. "It is inspiring to reflect that so masterly a building has been created in Dublin", he wrote. Though "completely modern in its

conception and method of construction... every particle down to the minutest detail has been selected and affixed with uttermost discrimination". The *Architectural Review* agreed that it was superbly built and sensuous in its surface texture as well as being dramatic and inflexible. Harry Allberry probably didn't know about one vignette, recalled with wry amusement by Paul Koralek: the sight of a donkey and cart

Visual essay 3: Light/Space
Ireland Frank McDonald

3.30

Visual essay 3: Light/Space
Ireland Frank McDonald

3.31

getting stuck in freshly-poured concrete
while the Library was being built. Or about
what happened the night before Eamon
deValera, then President of Ireland, was due
to turn the first sod, when some Trinity
students placed banana skins underneath it;
mercifully, they were found in time.

The Berkeley Library, officially opened by
deValera on July 12th, 1967, would rank on
anybody's "top twenty" of twentieth-century
buildings in Dublin. Yet when it came to
extending it, ABK – which had been
established on the strength of winning the
original competition – had to swallow the
bitter pill of losing out to McCullough Mulvin
(in association with Keane Murphy Duff) in a
limited competition held in 1997. ABK's
proposal was to put most of the extension
underground, beneath Fellows' Square, with
a slender glazed tower rising above it. But
this would have meant digging up the whole
square, which would have been hugely
disruptive to college activities – including
Trinity's lucrative tourist trade, centred on the
Book of Kells. So the easier option of
extending the Library towards Nassau Street
was chosen.

Inevitably, perhaps, this involved making
alterations to the Berkeley Library. It made
sense to use the existing portal as an

3.32

3.33

The deep window piercings in the facade of the Nebenzahl house are set at a variety of angles to filter the bright light characteristic of Jerusalem.

3.33

Aside from the exquisite effects of light on metal, the cladding of St Mary's Hospital was designed to provide maximum insulation for the walls and roof.

3.34

3.35
Strong daylight on the exterior of WH Smith's headquarters in Swindon, watched over by Elizabeth Frink's sculpture.

ABK designed a big new office building for WH Smith [of which Hornby was chairman] in Swindon. Dick Troughton and I insisted on 'good design'. I was furious about the Financial Times award which went to the Lloyd's building. WH Smith was the runner-up and should have won.

The project was for a headquarters building for our retail operations adjacent to, but not necessarily in keeping with our existing premises in Swindon. In our desire to have a proper building we were helped by Colin Amery who I had always known, and Hugh Casson who was a great friend. At that stage I spent more time with Richard Burton and I was particularly impressed with the hospital on the Isle of Wight. I can't remember who else we looked at, but we commissioned ABK as we liked them best.

I think we were good clients. We had regular meetings and Hugh Casson worked for us as a professional advisor to go through plans as well as our then chief architect David Baker and his deputy Peter Clapp. It was on time and on cost and we had great fun working with Peter Ahrends. He had clear ideas, he was adaptable but determined in issues that really mattered, and he also listened. It was not just design by management. We had staff working groups and thought about the inter-relationship between departments and communication.

It was built as a formation of cubes around courtyards with a corridor on a diagonal side spine. The design was expandable and Peter extended it about ten years after the first phase.

Overall we were delighted clients. ABK were delightful to work with.

Sir Simon Hornby

3.35

entrance to the whole library complex, rather than sidelining it altogether, so the route through the building had to be enlarged. And because it is cast in concrete, that solution was bound to do "a certain amount of violence to the building", as Paul Koralek said in his usual measured way. Engaged as a consultant on the project, he found himself involved in a damage limitation exercise: "It would have been unreasonable to say 'do nothing' because the problem would have come home to roost anyway ". A bigger threat was the fire officer's demand that the stairs and lobbies of the 1967 building should be enclosed.

Fellows' Square had, of course, been created by the construction of ABK's Arts and Social Sciences building in 1978. As architects of the Berkeley Library, the practice had been invited to take part in a "mini-competition" for this project nine years earlier. "My recollection is that we designed the TCD Arts Block on one of the station platforms in Reading while waiting for a train to London", says Peter Ahrends. When the proposals were discussed by the Faculty of Arts in 1969, according to Dr McParland, one speaker hoped that "blobs" such as those on the roof of the Library would not be a feature of the Arts Building; it was explained to him

3.37

3.36
By night, the Elizabeth Frink sculptures at WH Smith are individually lit, and further light spills out from the building.

3.37
The Kasmin Art Gallery in London was entered through a narrow corridor, lit subtly from above.

I was invited by Howard Goodman, Director of Health Building DHSS, to collaborate with Richard Burton in September 1983. The general brief I was given was "to look at the design for the new hospital and suggest ways in which the arts could be incorporated into it".

Working with Richard Burton was a great pleasure; from his personal experience of hospitals he knew that a well-designed and beautiful healthcare environment could be of real benefit to patients and staff.

Richard, Steve Nicoll the interior designer and myself developed a close understanding of what we believed should be achieved. We commissioned paintings, tapestries, murals, mobiles, ceramics and sculpture to enhance particular places within the building. Our plans made provision for exhibitions of arts and crafts and performances of music and theatre to become part of the ambience of the new hospital. Thousands of people queued to see the hospital for the first time – many said they wanted to see their contribution to the many artworks inside.

We considered the theme of water in all its form to be an appropriate starting point for the artworks. This theme pervades the building, both and out, in all shapes, colours and textures.

Peter Senior

3.38

that certain hydraulic equipment had to be housed on the roofs of modern buildings and that, in any case, Koralek, amongst others, was rather attached to "blobs".

The principal problem confronting the architects was how to increase the volume and density of the college to cater for a vastly expanded student population, while maintaining its established scale and character. This resulted in an unusually compact, deep-plan building, stepped in section to allow in light and air, and with its overall height restricted to below that of the Old Library directly opposite. The scheme was, nonetheless, controversial. Apart from weighty criticisms within Trinity, conservation groups outside joined battle by opposing the college's planning application, and the subsequent public hearing, as Dr McParland recalls, was "the arena for one of the most celebrated planning controversies of the 1970s". As a result, the architects had to refine and revise their scheme, to assuage some of the objections.

The accommodation is planned on five floors. The lower two levels contain the principal lecture theatres, including the 400-seat Edmund Burke Hall, the Lecky Library and coffee bar, all arranged around the main concourse. Upstairs are departmental offices

3.38
The facade of St Mary's Hospital continues to surprise, even after dark, when light leaks out from inside the building.

3.39
The dramatic articulation of Cummins Engines' window openings results in a spectacular and memorable night-time exterior.

3.39

and smaller teaching spaces, laid out in clusters around internal courts. The Douglas Hyde Gallery of Art is just inside the main entrance off Nassau Street. According to Dr McParland, the Arts Building, with its tumbling terraces softened by greenery, "lacks the finesse of Paul Koralek's Berkeley Library and is less well built". But the addition of a glazed and canopied sixth storey – "a big floating thing", as Koralek

describes it – should provide the building with a more eye-catching roofline, as well as much-needed space for endlessly growing student numbers. "The single most important thing we did in Trinity was to knock a hole in the railings on Nassau Street", says Koralek. "Nothing else we'll ever do will compare with that, because it suddenly made the place accessible by creating a route through it". The symbolism of opening up to the city was

particularly appropriate; four years earlier, in 1974, the Catholic ban had been lifted, changing Trinity's character forever.
    ABK's other noteworthy educational project in Dublin was St Andrew's College, in Booterstown, completed in 1972 – six years before Trinity's Arts Building. It gave the practice an opportunity to explore the philosophy of school design, to the extent that any architects could within the tight

St Andrew's College, Booterstown

budgetary constraints set by the Department of Education. And to a large extent, it succeeded. The brief required a secondary school for 300 pupils, a junior school for 100 and residential accommodation for boarders. Despite these disparate elements, all parts of the school were planned together in a single structure to encourage integration between seniors and juniors, day pupils and boarders. Teaching is done in a variety of spaces of

different size and character, each adjacent to a small garden court. This rejection of institutional norms gave the teaching areas an informality hitherto unknown in Irish schools, even though St Andrew's was organised on a quite rigid planning and structural module. The interior still works very well, some three decades later, though its joys can barely be imagined behind the rather drab, even forbidding, fair-faced

concrete block it presents to the world outside.

After completing the Arts Building in Trinity, work in Ireland dried up for ABK. The 1980s was a decade of recession and retrenchment, so there wasn't much happening anyway. Only one project materialised – a stone-faced house in the picturesque valley of Glencree, County Wicklow, just south of Dublin, a fine

Collaborations Paul Finch

The period during which ABK established itself as one of the country's foremost

practices was one which saw the gradual dilution of a command economy, culminating in the Thatcher years, where market forces ostensibly replaced the ethos of "the man in

3.40

Private house, Wicklow

Private house, Wicklow

Private house, Wicklow: central room

contemporary design built for a client who insisted on anonymity. But ABK's fortunes, so damaged in Britain by Prince Charles's egregious characterisation of their National Gallery extension as a "monstrous carbuncle", changed in Ireland after the practice was commissioned to renovate and extend the Dublin Dental Hospital in 1991. The dean, Professor Derry Shanley, who would have been well aware of ABK's early

masterpiece, the Berkeley Library, played a pivotal role in selecting the partnership for the £13 million project. Shanley was intent on transforming the shamefully-neglected, ramshackle hospital into a modern state-of-the-art facility next to Trinity's Lincoln Place gate and he was determined that it would be done with a certain panache. Or as Paul Koralek tells it, the dean of Trinity's Dental School "fell in love with our department store

for John Lewis" in Kingston upon Thames.
    One of the conditions of ABK's appointment was that the architects should set up a site office instead of flying in from London every week. Instead of being a burden, this proved to be a major boon because it gave the practice a physical presence in Dublin, and helped to generate Irish work. The Dental Hospital site office, headed by Paul de Freine, was replaced by a

Whitehall knows best". Like its contemporaries in private practice, ABK thus found itself in the philosophical no man's land of claiming, implicitly, greater skill and knowledge than that offered by public sector architects' departments, while being largely dependent on those self-same departments (or their municipal employers) for commissions. For 25 years, the relationship between the two sectors was well expressed in the RIBA's annual conferences. Public sector architects attended courtesy of their local authority – in those days happy to see their professionals attending events of this sort. Private sector architects attended at least partly in the hope of meeting potential future clients, or quasi-clients, in the form of those public sector professionals.

Dublin Dental Hospital   Dublin Dental Hospital   Dublin Dental Hospital

proper suite of offices in a Georgian house on Lower Leeson Street. John Parker came in from award-winning architects deBlacam and Meagher, and he was joined by Robert Davys, who had spent more than a decade with ABK, working on the British Embassy among other projects. Now, there is a staff of nine there.

The first phase of the Dental Hospital was a new building on its Trinity side, clad in granite like many of the college's other buildings, on a site adjoining the Department of Mechanical Engineering by Grafton Architects. Paul Koralek found the dialogue with them "fun to do", not least because it is quite unusual among architects. As a result, apart from the different roof treatments, the buildings line up perfectly. The new building was also designed to address a proposed square just inside Trinity's Lincoln Gate. Its circular tower, in glass block with steel finials, was intended to provide the hospital with "a landmark which people will get to recognise and know", according to Koralek. And, as with the earlier entrance through the Arts Building, he sees the Dental Hospital as another "interface between the city and the college".

A curved wall of red brick partially wraps around the tower, and there is an amazing

This same period was one in which a form of caste system operated within the architectural profession, whose psychological impact has only weakened during the last ten years. "System" is perhaps putting it too strongly, but there was most certainly an attitude on the part of "good" architects that they could leave commercial work to somebody else, whose skills would be less to do with design than with the ability to achieve planning permissions. The "commercial" firms, busy with an ever-growing market for offices, factory estates and shopping centres, generally for developer clients, felt they would never get a look-in (even if they wanted it) in the commissioning of health, educational and other public building types. Honours flowed

3.41

3.42
The lightness of form and structure in this competition entry for a bell tower in Canberra is accentuated by its reflection in the water below.

to the "good" architects, while their commercial non-rivals found satisfaction from the considerable fees to be earned at a time when clients expected to pay their architect on the basis of the RIBA fee scale.

Such a world is already beginning to appear remote: no fee bids, everyone more or less abiding by RIBA codes in respect of how they won commissions and how they were rewarded. Not surprisingly, given that a client would pay roughly the same fee whichever

architect he ended up using, one common way in which architects were chosen was through personal relationships – hence the phrase "golf-club architects". Eric Lyons, a witty RIBA president, once quipped that under the institute's rules, you could not

Dublin Dental Hospital, treatment suite   Dublin Dental Hospital, atrium

view of its slim profile, just nine inches thick and rising to four storeys, as one passes by. It also "cleans up the corner visually", as Koralek says, though the overall effect would have been more pleasing if Flemish rather than stretcher bond had been used for the brickwork. Unfortunately, the budget didn't allow for "extras". It was also a very difficult site. "Part of the problem was how to end up with a single building, rather than an old

building and a splendid new one, so somehow merging it into a single entity was very high on our priority list", according to the architect. Some would argue that ABK's design team didn't quite pull this off; visually, the architectural treatment reads as three separate elements rather than a unified whole.

The facade of the new building, facing north into the college, is very contemporary

in style. Its ground floor has the solidity appropriate to a base, with small window openings to give some privacy to patients in the main operating theatre as well as the accident and emergency clinic. Above it are the main dental clinics – the very raison d'etre of the hospital, which is about treating patients and teaching students. Here, in the bright and cleverly laid out interior, the privacy of patients is protected by panels tied

solicit for business, "but you could loiter with intent at the 19th".

ABK had no need of golf clubs. Many of their most substantial commissions came from personal recommendations or success in competitions, the latter being another key way in which clients could get the best design for the same fee as an inferior one, and moreover find out in advance what they would be paying for. By and large (with one highly important exception), the work ABK won in competition ended up being built – not something one could guarantee about competitions today. (Paul Koralek was closely involved with the running and judging of the abortive Cardiff Bay Opera House competition in 1995.)

The assumption that a competition would

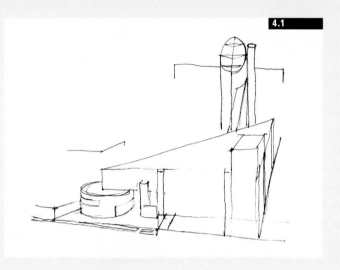

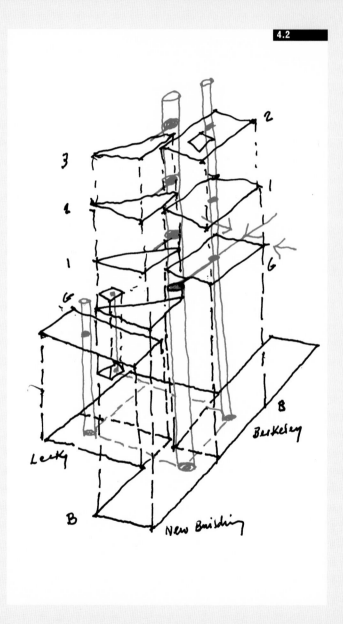

National Gallery extension, Dublin

Liffey Bridge competition

to a steel screen which the architect likens to "lace curtains on a parlour window". To avoid the "nightmare scenario" of row upon row of chairs, ABK devised a triangular module, based on the fact that dentists "are really only interested in one end of a person", without compromising the overall sense of space. The main device to link clinical facilities in the new building and teaching facilities in the old one is a rectangular atrium, which rises to four storeys under a glazed roof. This is a very impressive space and one is immediately struck by its quality of light, so starkly different to the hospital's dingy past, and by its cantilevered stainless steel-railed staircase with round-ended landings, one stepped back from the other.

In 1996, two years before the Dental Hospital was finally completed, ABK were among the twelve firms of international architects invited to participate in a competition to design an extension to the National Gallery of Ireland for a site on Clare Street, across from the hospital. Their design, with its huge corniced parapet, lost out to Benson and Forsyth, in what turned out to be a tortuous project for the winners. ABK did even better in a 1998 competition for the design of a new footbridge across the Liffey to celebrate the Millennium, making it to the

in fact result in a building was an important one for both client and architect: it meant the client was seeking an architect and a design in order to start work, not in order to avoid or delay making a decision. For the architect, it meant the hours of unpaid work (in the case of open competitions) or low-paid work (for invited competitions) could be justified by the prospect of real buildings at the end of the process – assuming your designs were good enough.

While the precise form of each competition might differ, it was generally to find a design rather than a friendly face. There was, by definition, an assumption that if you were good enough to win a competition, you were good enough to see it through: you were not expected to have designed 50 libraries to

4.1
A conceptual sketch for the Berkeley Library extension competition.

4.2
Three-dimensional study of the principal elements in the proposed extension.

4.3
Interior view of the reading room with its glazed roof.

4.4
A new plaza lying between the Berkeley Library, the Arts Faculty Building and the library extension.

4.3

4.4

Institute of Technology, Tralee

Institute of Technology, Tralee

Institute of Technology, Tralee

final shortlist. But their proposal to suspend the deck from a pair of steel masts on each side of the river was pipped at the post by Dublin-based architects Howley Harrington (with Price and Myers), whose entry was more deferential to the nearby Ha'penny Bridge (1815).

A foothold was established in Waterford when ABK was commissioned to convert a 200-year-old quayside granary into a visitor centre and tourist office. Two of the existing low-headroom floors were removed to form three floors of multimedia exhibition space; on a later visit, Peter Ahrends was horrified to discover that swagged drapes and candelabra had been added to the Granary's glazed café. Also in 1998, ABK produced a new masterplan for the development of Waterford Institute of Technology, which would involve creating a curvaceous band of buildings to enclose the existing pre-cast blocks dating from the late–1960s. But this, and a circular canopied structure as well as a series of pools to add "sparkle" to the campus, was probably too radical for the authorities to take on board. So the plan "faded".

The practice has also prepared a development plan for the Institute of Technology in Tralee, County Kerry, which

prove you could design a good one. It may seem curious, given the supposed culture of risk-taking established in Britain post–Margaret Thatcher, but looking at the history of ABK's earlier buildings, it is apparent that clients were prepared to take (no doubt calculated) risks in their choice of architect which they might not do today. There was surely, in the minds of clients still conscious of the Second World War, an acknowledgement of the achievements and responsibilities of the very young – during military service. ABK's partners were too young to have been involved in the war, but when they entered the Architectural Association in 1951, the director of the Festival of Britain, Hugh Casson, was only 43. There was some risk-taking. AA graduates

4.5
Masterplan for the University of Grenoble, which places a series of new buildings on a clearly-articulated urban axis.

4.6
A sketch of one of the buildings on the axis.

4.7
The Grenoble masterplan proposal includes an inhabited bridge, an idea under development in this sketch.

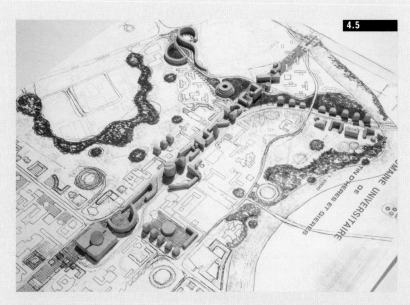

Institute of Technology, Blanchardstown

Civic centre, Offaly

is relocating to an elevated site of 60 acres outside this booming town. New buildings for business studies, information technology and hotel management have already been completed to a curved plan and scheme designs done for a library, student services building, sports centre and other facilities. ABK have made an even bigger splash with the Institute of Technology on a 45-acre greenfield site in Blanchardstown, a fast-developing area on the edge of Dublin, seven miles north-west of the city centre. It is regarded as the flagship project which should provide an exemplary basis for the development of a much larger business park by IDA Ireland, the state-sponsored industrial development authority. Located to the north of A+D Wejchert's Blanchardstown shopping centre, the first phase of the campus has been completed to ABK's design and masterplan. The new buildings – a library, a multi-purpose hall with catering facilities and accommodation for general teaching and training – are quite dramatic architecturally, curved in plan with external circular concrete columns supporting canopied roofs.

Another growth area for ABK in Ireland has been the design of civic offices for local authorities. Offaly County Council

4.7

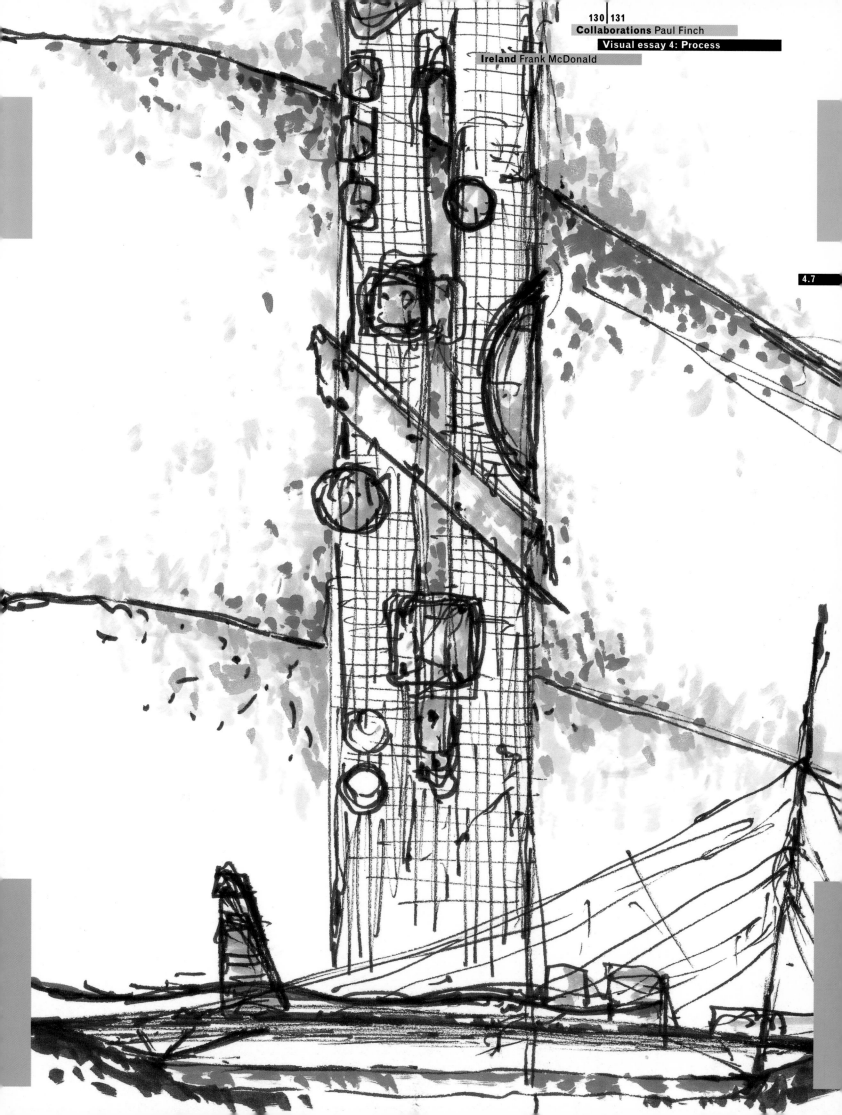

Powell & Moya were working on their competition-winning design for the Churchill Gardens estate in Pimlico – having built nothing before. (On learning that the winners were more or less students, the client for that project, Westminster Council, responded by promising them the best consultant they could find to work with them. Days of hope...)

A decade later, when ABK came to national prominence, the role of client and architect had settled comfortably into its ambiguous public/private relationship. The speculative property boom of the Harold Wilson governments in the 1960s had yet to happen, but days of materials shortages and endless permits to do almost anything had come to an end (the only exception being exchange controls, which lasted until 1979 and surely

4.8

4.8
Careful detailing of the construction elements at DLR stations is designed to be used as a kit of parts for all stations.

4.9
The pedestrian bridge at Poplar, with lightweight steel girders supporting curved glass panels.

Civic centre, Tipperary

commissioned a new headquarters for a well-chosen site in Tullamore, near the courthouse and railway station. The project consists of a three-storey energy-efficient office building, divided into two halves by a central concourse which will provide both daylight and natural ventilation. Conceived as a pavilion in a mature Victorian garden with some extraordinarily fine trees, the main elevations are clad in timber and glass and surrounded by a slatted timber screen, to give shading and a sense of depth. This "trellis of timber", as John Parker describes it, wrapping around what is essentially a concrete-framed glass box, is intended to integrate the building with its verdant setting. Unfortunately, many of the trees are in poor health and will need to be replaced.

The civic offices in Nenagh for Tipperary (North Riding) County Council, Nenagh Urban District Council and the local health board are just two storeys high. Designed to provide a "one-stop shop" for public services, the building is organised around a double-height central concourse, with three wings of offices on one side, services on the other and, at the front, council chambers for the two local authorities. For Limerick County Council, ABK did a feasibility study for housing on a 14-acre site at the edge of

4.9

inhibited UK architects from undertaking work abroad). Over the next 25 years, ABK were to embark on a series of architectural journeys, for a wide variety of clients, investigating and innovating to an unusual extent across an equally wide range of

building types. Can we find points in common, not in respect of the architectural thinking, but of the clients?

Perhaps the first thing to observe is that almost all of them wanted buildings for their use, rather than to lease or sell on to others.

By and large, ABK's relationship to speculation has been intellectual and architectural. Although occasional commissions came from the property sector, the iconic speculative office building is one of the few building types missing from the firm's impressive canon.

4.10
The steel and glass tube of Poplar Bridge is supported by a simple cable-stay structure.

4.11
Drawing of details in a DLR viaduct station, including staircase and lift access from street level.

4.12
Design drawing for Poplar Bridge, including details of cable-stay fixings.

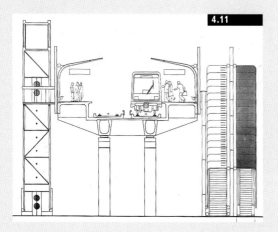

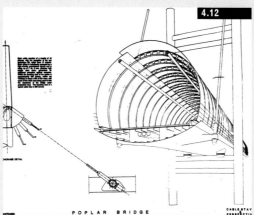

POPLAR BRIDGE

Carrickmines Croquet and Tennis Club: rendering

Carrickmines Club: facade detail

Newcastle West and were then commissioned to design a first phase of 50 units. Drawing on and re-interpreting the Irish vernacular tradition, the terraced two-storey houses are laid out in crescents around landscaped public spaces – much like Frank Gibney's superb estate villages for Bord na Mona. By contrast with most speculatively-built private housing, the scheme incorporates high levels of insulation

and draught minimisation, as well as taking orientation into account for passive solar gain and the availability of light, so important in Ireland during the winter. It was also designed for lifetime use, with the provision of a ground-floor toilet in each house. Parking is arranged in cobbled bays at the front.

The Carrickmines Croquet and Tennis Club, in a salubrious area of south County Dublin, presented quite a different problem – how to

mask three large indoor tennis courts to retain the domestic "home away from home" scale members wanted for their clubhouse. This conundrum was resolved by John Parker by reforming the landscape and wrapping the clubhouse around the front and side of the courts. The result is "a stepped prairie house with, perhaps, a prairie barn behind", according to Robert Bevan, in *BD Ireland*. The projecting timber-clad corner window and

Another client reference point is the high proportion that were public sector or quasi-public sector organisations. At the time this was entirely normal – Britain going through an intimate courtship and marriage with welfarism, ending in the divorce of 1979. It is worth remarking on that proportion in the light of conditions today, where architects including ABK have had to establish new relationships with quite different 'clients' in order to design public buildings. New forms of procurement, such as the 'public private partnership', or the 'private finance initiative' were unknown for most of ABK's output from the 1960s to the 1990s.

Another seam running through the practice's oeuvre is education, beginning with that first competition win, the Trinity

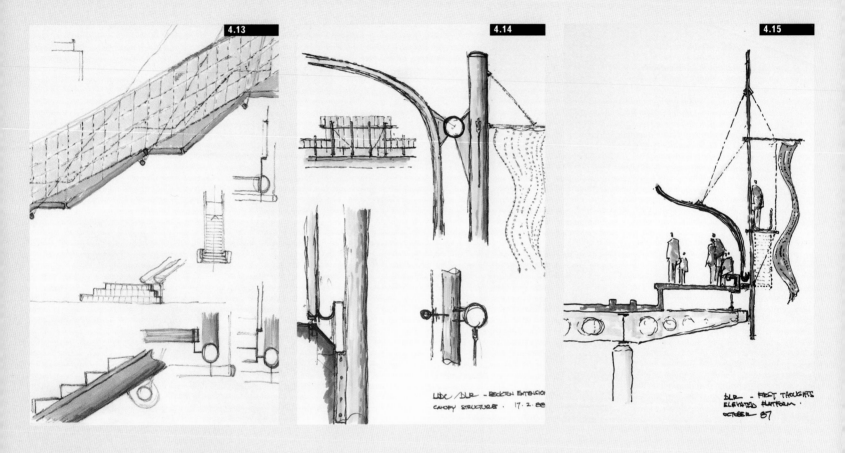

the pivoting or sliding room dividers are all deBlacam and Meagher-ish touches in this modest, but modern IR£2.7 million development.

ABK's engagement with Ireland has also led to a commission from the Dublin City Architect, Jim Barrett, to prepare a development plan for an entire city block in Sean MacDermott Street, in the hitherto neglected north-east inner city. Centred on a Victorian convent building, which is to be reconstituted, this pump-priming exercise may include a tall residential tower, a series of mixed use buildings and a civic centre. But the practice's most significant Irish project, potentially, is a commission from Trinity College to prepare a development pan for the proposed Dublin Docklands Innovation Centre on Pearse Street and design its first phase. Covering virtually an entire city block, from Macken Street to Grand Canal Quay, the site is currently occupied by a college-owned enterprise centre which was developed by IDA Ireland in the 1980s. The sharp red-brick

College Dublin library. Other libraries followed, as did designs for schools and universities; at a more general level there are museums, galleries, heritage centres. It is learning, as well as the public sector, which provides the best area of client connectivity.

This is not to ignore achievements in other areas – another characteristic of ABK's work is the engagement with a particular building type, significant achievement, but then little else in that field. Examples include the factory for Cummins Engines, the Moscow Embassy, the Habitat Warehouse, John Lewis department store and the Isle of Wight hospital: set pieces of a high order into which considerable architectural and other forms of research were undertaken. Why not more repeat buildings? Perhaps because, like other

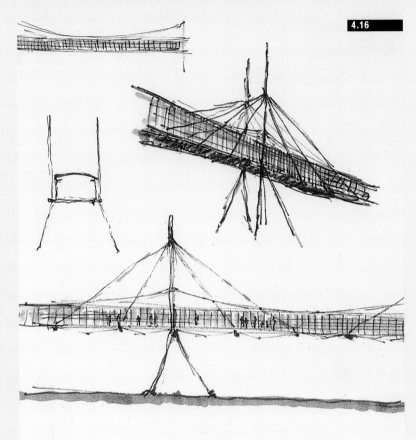

4.16

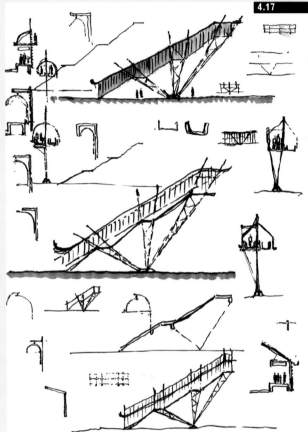

4.17

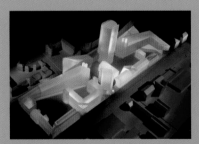

Convent Lands, Dublin: model

complex won several awards at the time, but its low-rise scale is now seen as out of kilter with the goal of developing more densely in the Docklands area. The only truly outstanding building on the site, a stone-clad former sugar refinery, is bound to be retained in the redevelopment programme; indeed, its height – at seven storeys – is likely to provide a benchmark for the new buildings.

ABK's founders have always been enthusiastic about working in Ireland. "There's a certain element of chaos here that I find appealing", Peter Ahrends says. "In some respects, it's more radical. And the poetic dimension of Irish life and culture puts architects in a position more analogous to Europe than Britain; there is an acceptance that, as an architect, you have a voice in the making of contemporary culture". Some might dismiss this as an overly positive assessment, particularly as the absence of registration of title still means that anyone in Ireland can call himself, or herself, an architect. But at least the country is not

4.18

dominated by any equivalent of the British establishment or heritage lobby "hanging onto the past like no right-minded Irishman would ever want to do", as Paul Koralek puts it; things are more fluid in Ireland. Much of ABK's work is now being done in their busy Dublin office, and this is likely to continue for at least as long as Ireland's so-called Celtic Tiger economy.

practitioners of their generation, ABK have had little interest in, or aptitude for, the kind of "marketing" required to win commissions which involve off-the-peg repetition rather than new challenges, new thinking, and new clients.

A final characteristic is that very rarely does an ABK project involve a significant mixture of uses, or of clients; even where there is a mix, it is usually of related activities, within a dental hospital or an arts faculty, for instance. This puts in perspective

the saga of the National Gallery Extension project; this traumatic episode should not overshadow the practice's achievements, and one should remember that ABK's biggest project, the Moscow Embassy, post-dates it. However, the bizarre and scandalous

4.19

4.20

4.18
Poplar Bridge at night.

4.19
A full-sized prototype for the DLR canopy structure.

4.20
Poplar Bridge is currently incomplete. It has been fitted with a glazed end and a temporary staircase, both of which are planned for removal.

treatment of the architect illuminates the complexities and contradictions surrounding what should have been a high-point in the practice's history. A taste of things to come was Peter Ahrends being told that, although ABK had won the competition, "We don't like your building" – or words to that effect. An account of the competition and its aftermath appears elsewhere in this volume; these are some general observations about client/architect relations in the 1980s – the Thatcher decade – and the climate in which those relationships flourished or foundered.

Despite much that has been written about Margaret Thatcher, she was no enemy of great public buildings, or indeed of great public projects. Her praise for the French *grands projets* programme may be said to

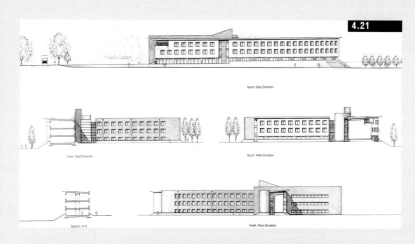

4.21
Studies for the facades at Loughborough University Business School and Economics Building.

4.22
The white-rendered curved facade houses a business school and management development centre. The colour reflects the sun's heat.

4.23
A model of the building shows the different elements of the building, each articulated by coloured render.

4.24
The northern facade of the business school is in terracotta render to relate to adjacent early 20th-century brick 'academic tudor' buildings.

4.25
A sketch study for Worcester Hospital.

have set in train the creation of the Lottery, and the building of the greatest wave of UK cultural buildings in Britain for a century. Her support for the redevelopment of London's Docklands was, coincidentally, to make possible ABK's Docklands Light Railway extension project. It also resulted in the Jubilee Line Extension and a major road programme to service, in particular, Canary Wharf. Thatcher also backed the Channel Tunnel project, signing the historic agreement with François Mitterrand.

But it is also true that she had an aversion to paying for public facilities if there were any chance of somebody else footing the bill. (One of the things she liked about the Channel Tunnel project was that it was privately funded.) Under Thatcher's

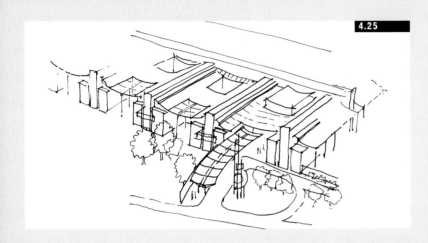

4.25

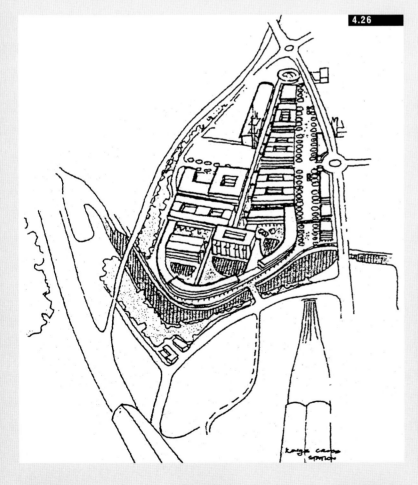

4.26

4.27

The Millennium Hospital—View from gateway of the main entrance. 25.11.97. AO.

4.28

4.26
Sketch for the Millennium Hospital, which would have used a brownfield site and 'air rights' space behind King's Cross Station.

4.27
The main entrance to the Millennium Hospital, with no hint of the busy railway lines which run underneath the building.

4.28
Perspective view of Worcester Hospital.

4.29

4.29

The woodland setting for Hooke
Park College in Dorset provides
the raw material for two
buildings ABK developed there,
using unsawn round timber.

premiership the Treasury began to rethink the rules on public/private financing. She was also a great proselytiser for self-help. This attitude of "public equals bad, private equals good", was to have malign consequences. Where prime ministers lead, others follow. Cultural institutions began to believe that the only way to attract government funding for building projects was to sell off their own assets to prove their worthiness. Should not property assets owned by these institutions be exploited to help their finances? (That is why the BBC was to abandon its Norman Foster-designed headquarters scheme in Langham Place in favour of a second-rate building in White City, and a property deal in which the developer did considerably better than the corporation.)

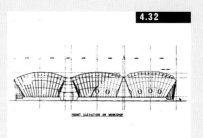

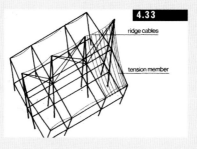

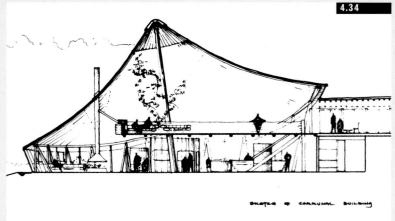

4.30
A study model for the workshop at Hooke Park, showing how the softwood roof structure is anchored at each side.

4.31
Hooke Park workshop, sketch elevations.

4.32
Structure study for the workshop and residence at Hooke Park.

In the case of the National Gallery, the trustees were headed by the formidable Lord Annan (if there were a committee of the great and the good, he would have chaired it). Despite being of high intellect and high achievement, they somehow reached the conclusion that the way to pay for an extension was to incorporate a commercial property development. Since they knew nothing about development, the trustees opted for a developer/architect form of competition – a notoriously difficult competition type because there is in-built ambiguity about whether you want the best design, or the best commercial deal. It was a very big mistake for one simple reason: the site was simply not large enough to do all that would undoubtedly be required, if not

4.33
Structure study for the workshop and residence at Hooke Park.

4.34
Study for the communal building at Hooke Park.

4.35
Site progress at the workshop, with wetwood timber members fixed in place.

4.36
The interior of the workshop, whose roof is punctured along the crown of the arch by glazed panels.

4.37
Site progress at the residence.

immediately, then at some time in the future. The real challenge of the project, providing a magnificent addition to William Wilkins' half-baked building, was diluted by the need to think about office development.

Into this quagmire of mixed use and property development stepped ABK. Their developer client, Nigel Broackes of Trafalgar House, was not the sort of client the architects were used to dealing with. A ruthless operator in the world of property, construction and shipping, Broackes was a capitalist red in tooth and claw, ex-public school and Army. His side-kick, Victor Matthews, was the cheese to his chalk-stripe, a building worker made good, unkindly satirised by Private Eye as "Sid Whelks".

4.38
This model shows ABK's original development plan for Hooke Park, including several buildings which were not eventually completed.

4.39
The memorable gable and red detailing on the residence have helped the building become one of Hooke Park's better-known icons.

4.40
The unfinished interior of the residence.

4.41
The glazed gable end of the workshop building brings light and air into the interior.

They were about as far removed from Trinity College Dublin as one could imagine. Nevertheless, something worked, and the competition was won, against a shortlist including SOM and Richard Rogers. The competition was controversial, but nobody could have guessed how much more controversial it was to become.

To say that the heir to the throne dropped a bombshell on the British architectural establishment in May 1984 would be putting it mildly. Prince Charles chose the occasion of the 150th anniversary celebrations of the RIBA, held at Hampton Court, to launch his carefully prepared attack on Modernism and all its works. In singling out two unbuilt proposals for particular criticism, neither of which had planning permission, Charles was

4.41

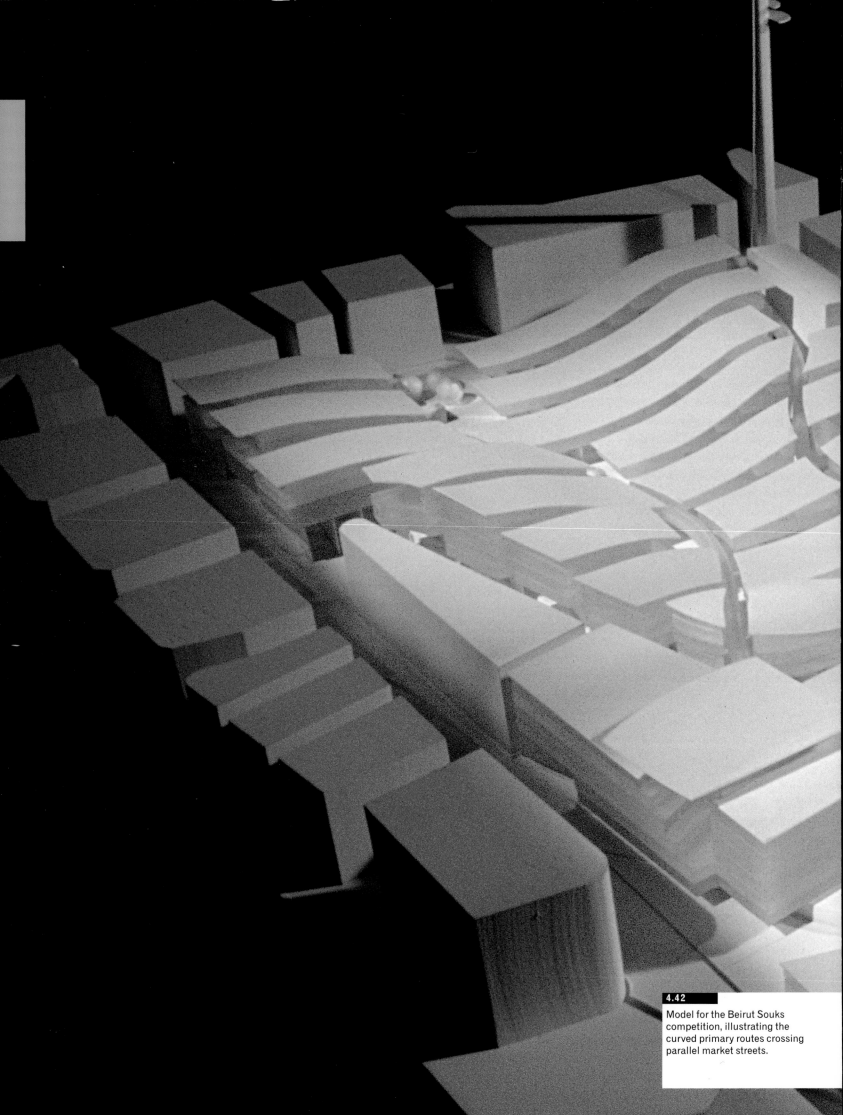

4.42
Model for the Beirut Souks
competition, illustrating the
curved primary routes crossing
parallel market streets.

4.42

treading on dangerous ground. The Secretary of State for the Environment, Patrick Jenkin, was present at the speech, and as the man responsible for all planning permis-sion was clearly appalled by what had been said. He assured an ashen-faced Peter Palumbo, developer of the Mies van der Rohe tower and square in the City of London (or "glass stump" as the Prince put it, "better suited to downtown Chicago"), that the forth-coming public inquiry would be dealt with absolutely impartially, despite the Prince's comments.

For ABK and Trafalgar House, the last thing they needed was royal criticism. Charles' famous one-liner, that the design was a "monstrous carbuncle" (on the face of a much-loved and elegant friend) had been borrowed from a novelette by his wife's

4.43

1:500

4.44

WATER FLOW - SOUK ROUTE

A partnership of three excep-tionally talented architects, who also happen to be extremely good, caring and decent people and which survives the trials and vicissitudes of more than four decades in joint practice must be a rarity if not unique. Good, let alone great architecture in more often than not an individualistic, if not an egocentric activity, yet Paul, Peter and Richard have managed to work together and create work of great distinction since the day they decided to leave employment and set up on their own.

I first met Peter through knowing and working with his father. Steffen Ahrends was a distinguished architect who emigrated from Europe to South Africa in the 1930s. In 1957 his son Peter, having graduated at London's Architectural Association, came to Johannesburg to work with his Dad and it was then that I first met this young, tall, handsome, courteous and talented architect.
We started working together shortly after the three musketeers had started their own firm back in London. I helped them with a

competition for a Carillon to be erected by Lake Burley Griffin in Canberra, a splendid concept which I still believe should have won. Paul Koralek was the partner responsible for the project and my Australian partner always thought he could have passed as my (much) younger brother. Although Paul was making the running, I was struck by their cohesion, their togetherness, which they have never lost.
Collaborating with them individually and collectively on many projects has never been

dull, ever invigorating and stimulating in setting one's sights that notch higher. There is much idealism in their collective work which has maintained standards of integrity, excellence and personal commitment – a quite extraordinary partnership.

Jack Zunz

step-mother, Dame Barbara Cartland, and had about the same level of intellectual rigour. The word "carbuncle" rapidly became short-hand for any building which anyone disliked.

By the time of the Prince's intervention, the competition-winning design had been substantially amended to produce (pre-dictably) much more space than had been required by the original brief. The formal geo-metry of the original was diluted and a "tower" added; the scheme was subsequently called in for public inquiry and, like the Mies tower, was turned down by the Secretary of State. The gallery trustees started again: new brief, new architect, no offices. Robert Venturi, high priest of Post-Modernism, was eventually appointed. Was that what the Prince had wanted?

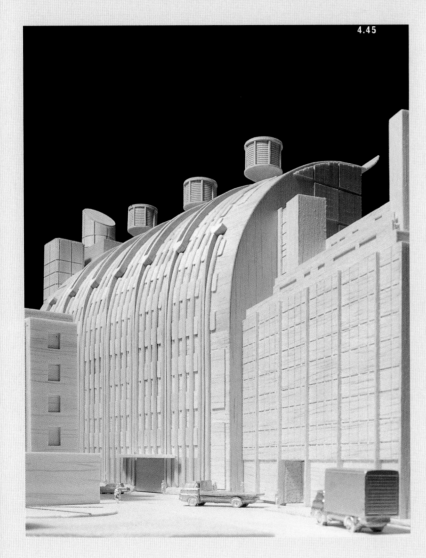

4.43
Conceptual sketch for the Beirut Souks competition, addressing the valley section of the buildings.

4.44
Conceptual sketch for the Beirut Souks competition.

4.45
Model showing ABK's proposal for Standard Life Development Offices in Shaftesbury Avenue, London.

4.46
The Shaftesbury Avenue proposal was to respond to adjacent buildings in a confined city-centre location.

4.47
A proposed office development of two related buildings at Chiswick Park in west London.

The worst thing about this disgraceful episode was that it made good architects like ABK (and subsequently James Stirling, whose design for Peter Palumbo replaced the Mies scheme) the whipping boys for third-rate commercial Modernism which had wrecked towns and cities all over Britain in the previous two decades. What the Prince had failed to understand was that ABK represented the antithesis of a repetitious, bastardised International Style. Their "Neo-Classical" competition entry was as unexpected in its plan form as anything the practice had previously produced. The architects were in a curious British vice: just when you thought you had identified a client, along came someone else with a greater claim. Who were ABK working for? The

4.48

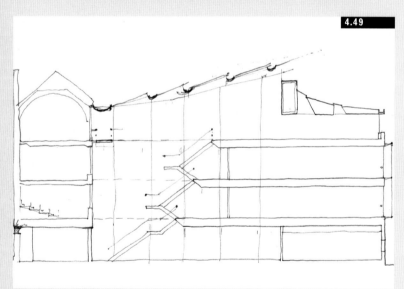

4.49

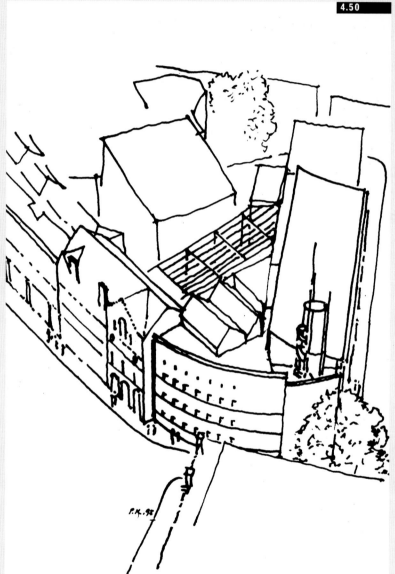

4.50

4.48
The original building on the site of the Dublin Dental Hospital was to be retained and enhanced by ABK's new design.

4.49
An early design section for the Dental Hospital illustrates how the new building responds to the historic building.

4.50
This perspective sketch for the Dental Hospital illustrates the junction of new and old buildings, with a progression of three new elements.

4.51
Interior view of the completed atrium at the Dental Hospital.

4.51

visiting public? Trafalgar House? The National Gallery Trustees? The planning authority? The Secretary of State for the Environment? The Prince of Wales?

The shock waves of Hampton Court and the National Gallery marked an end to an architectural age of innocence. The public sector was already reviled for the perceived and real failures of 1960s system-built housing. Now the leading lights of the profession were in the firing line. With fee scales crumbling and still under fire from a consumerist, free-market ethos, with contractual arrangements in flux, and with government funding regimes moving towards a "cheapest is best" attitude, the world of practice into which ABK had entered 25 years earlier was irrevocably changing.

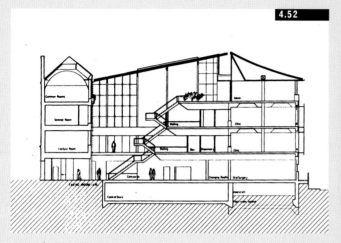

4.52

4.54

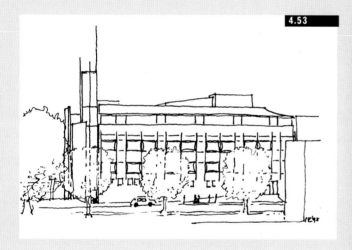

4.53

4.55

Rebuilding the Dublin Dental Hospital was first mooted in the 1940s, but the project did not come to fruition until 1994, when the government provided £7.5 million for new clinical facilities and the refurbishment of the Victorian building. Having waited 50 years for a decision to replace the building, the staff of the Dental Hospital had aspirations for this to be a model for other dental hospitals, despite the modest budget.

ABK had the task of designing a state-of-the-art facility in a confined and difficult site. What they achieved is recognised as one of the jewels in the College. The Dublin Dental Hospital has been cited as an example of how modest resources can be used effectively by ingenious architects to fulfil the fundamental requirements of firmness, commodity, and delight in a building.

Few could have anticipated the positive atmosphere that developed between the project team, led by Paul Koralek, and the future users. It seemed every person in the School and Hospital played a significant part in some facet of the design.

Everything we asked for from a functional perspective was provided, but we could not have anticipated such a delightful environment to house those activities as ABK provided for us. Four years after opening, the building continues to delight.
Derry Shanley

4.52

A more developed section through the stepped formation of the atrium at the Dental Hospital clearly shows the new and old buildings.

Happily, their values remained intact.

ABK's collaborations have generally been happy ones. If the clients weren't quite sure what sort of building would emerge as a result of the creative process, they were happy to trust their architect. This was certainly the case in respect of clients as varied as Terence Conran (Habitat), Derry Shanley (Dublin Dental Hospital) and Mark Bertram (Foreign & Commonwealth Office). Artists such as Tess Jaray have enjoyed the collaborations which Richard Burton has famously encouraged through his work at the Arts Council and elsewhere.

As for professional relationships, perhaps the most important has been with Ove Arup & Partners (as is true of so many practices). One vignette of how engineering and

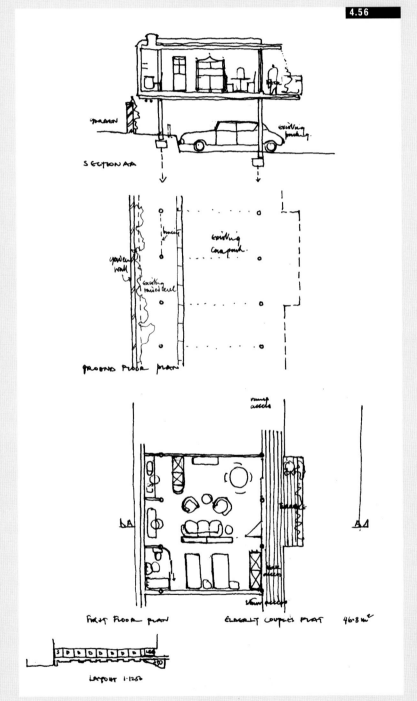

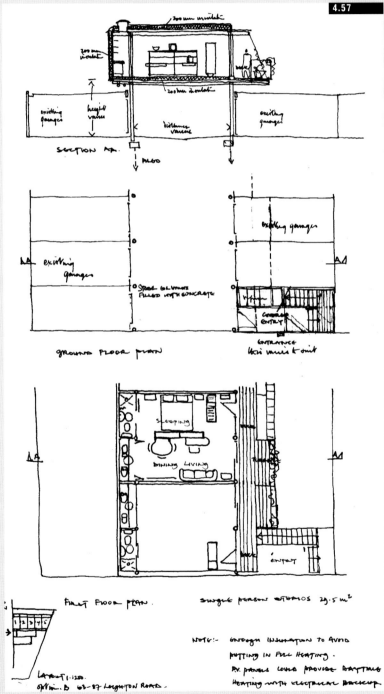

architecture sometimes fuse is provided in an early drawing for the first Moscow embassy design. Glance quickly and it might be the Terry Farrell Embankment Place project. In fact Richard Burton had studied the site as part of his work on regenerating the South Bank and connections (carried out with Richard Rogers) some while before the Farrell project was commissioned. Ideas about building above Charing Cross Station derived from the structural analysis by Arup, showing the optimum use of columns in relation to the platform below. As it turned out, Moscow went through two more evolutions before the final (different) design was achieved.

Finally, what of the most important professional collaboration of all: the practice

4.58

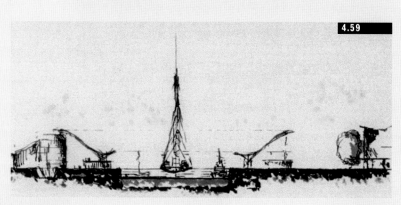

4.59

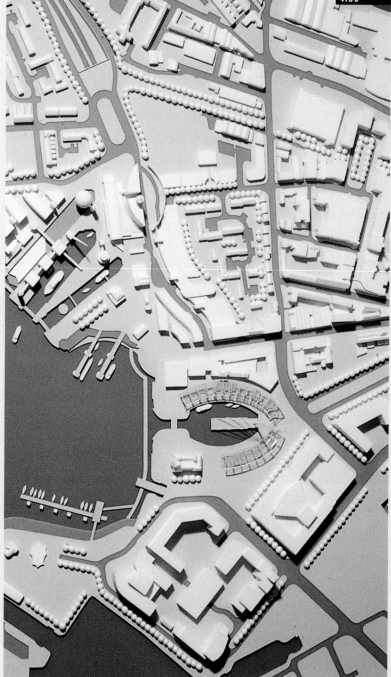

4.60

4.58
ABK's Techniquest building was completed, re-using the frame of an old industrial building.

4.59
ABK prepared a masterplan for Cardiff Bay Inner Harbour, a project including the old Oval Basin dock area.

4.60
The masterplan proposed the termination of a light rail system on a structure suspended over the Oval Basin.

4.61
To the west of London's Paddington station, a site known as North Pole was developed for servicing and repairing Eurostar trains.

4.62
ABK's proposed designs for the North Pole site provided train sheds where the work would take place.

itself? Each building is a separate story, and the roll-call of past and present contributors to the office is an impressive one. At their heart is the relationship between the three partners, three distinct personalities with as many differences as things in common.

Although particular buildings are associated with particular partners, it is inevitable that working together for four decades has resulted in a shorthand between them, common experiences and points of reference which will be mysterious to outsiders. Their

personalities are quite distinct, as have been their interests in architecture beyond the office, and one could not assume unanimity of reaction to particular problems or necessarily strategies for dealing with them. One can imagine Richard Burton getting

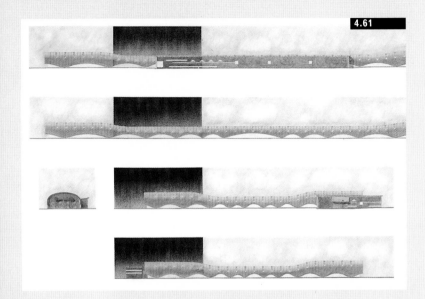

4.61

4.62

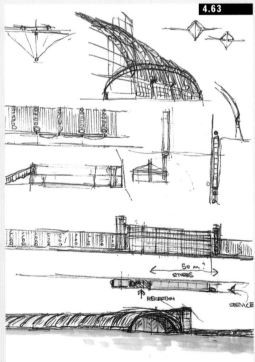

4.63

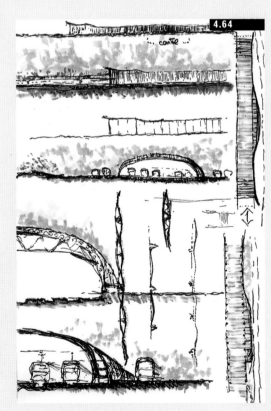

4.64

4.63

Reminiscent of the designs for Hooke Park, the train sheds at North Pole consisted of four cast arched steel structures.

4.64

Early sketches examined the options for achieving the defined functions on a tightly-confined site.

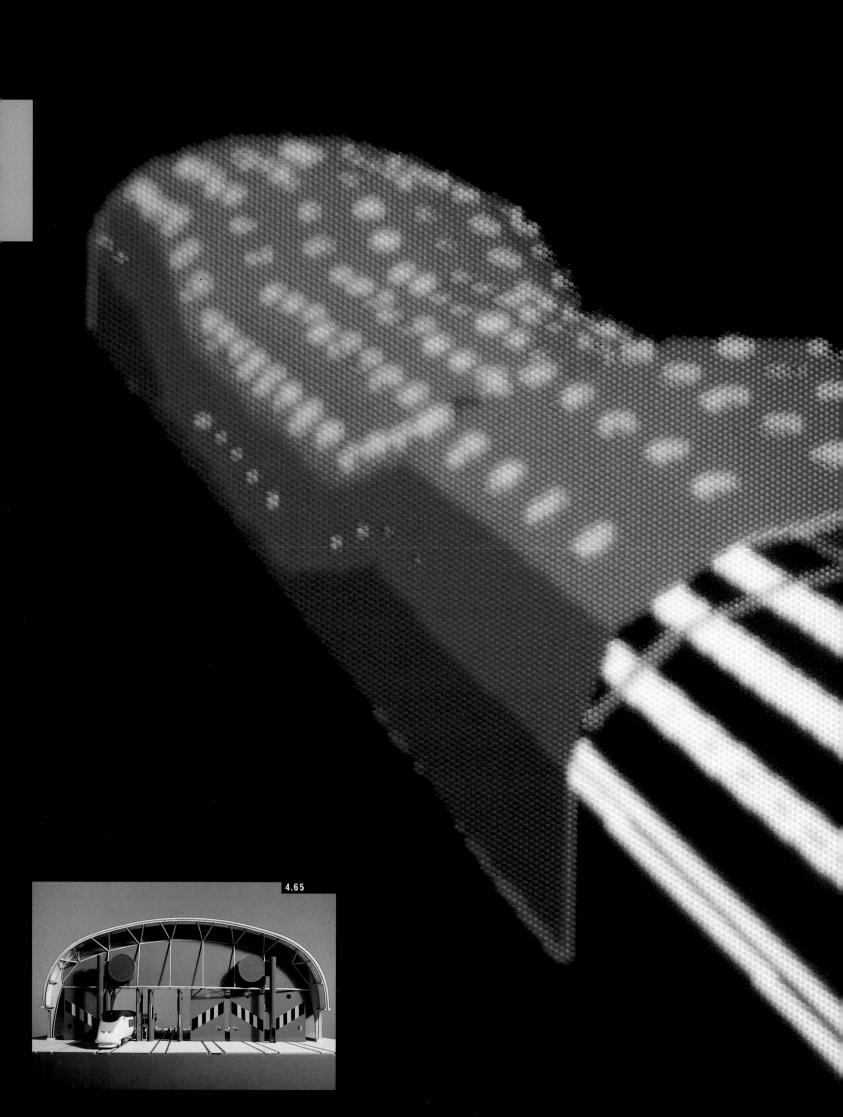

4.65

4.66

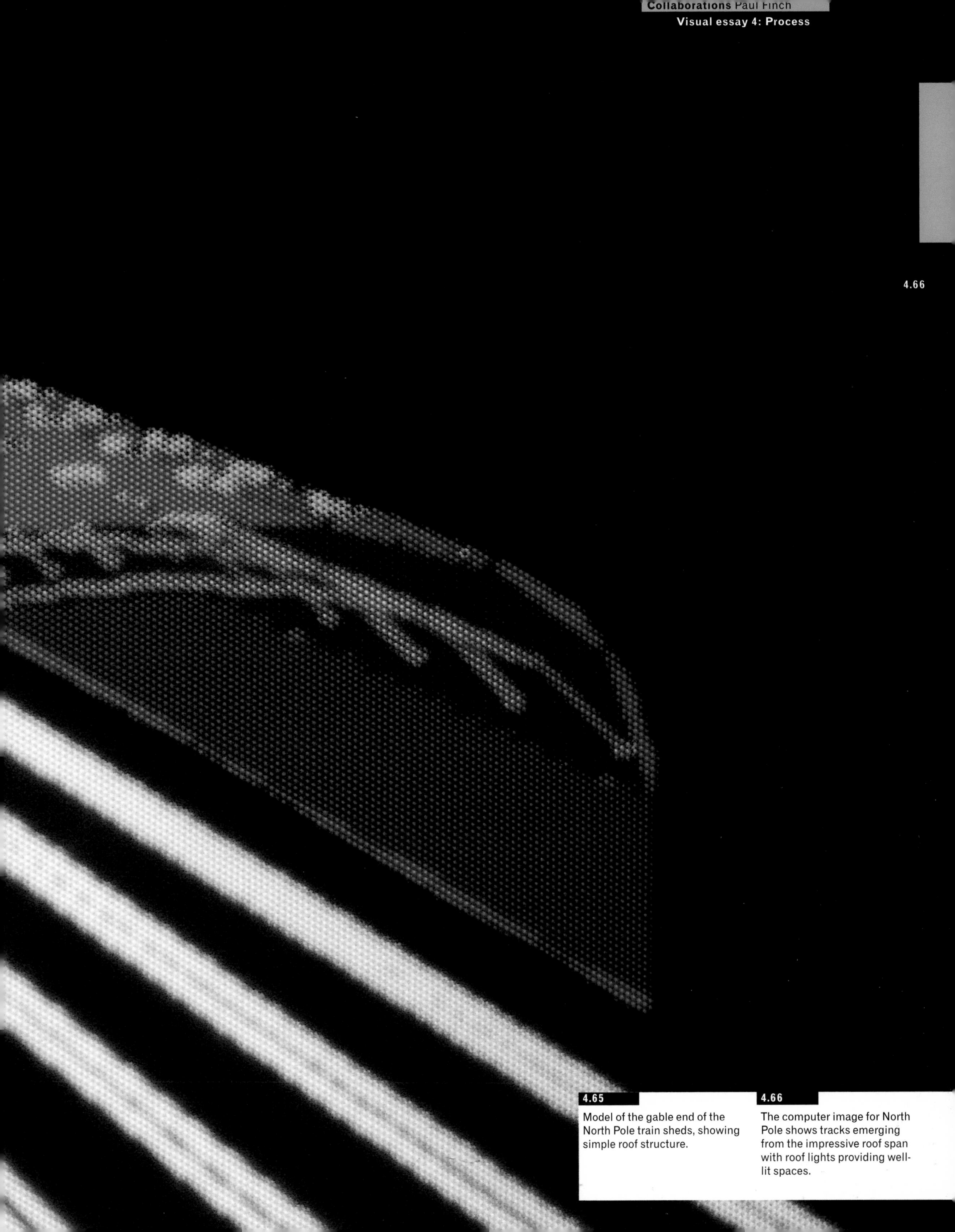

Model of the gable end of the
North Pole train sheds, showing
simple roof structure.

4.66

The computer image for North
Pole shows tracks emerging
from the impressive roof span
with roof lights providing well-
lit spaces.

ready to sound the drum, while Paul Koralek ponders on the nature of the drum and Peter Ahrends wonders whether actually a trumpet would be more appropriate.

If one were to look for a single word to summarise the nature of their collaborations and, most important, the built outcomes, I would choose "unpredictable", in its most constructive and positive sense. You expect the work to be interesting and good – without ever being able to predict what you are going to get, whatever the building type.

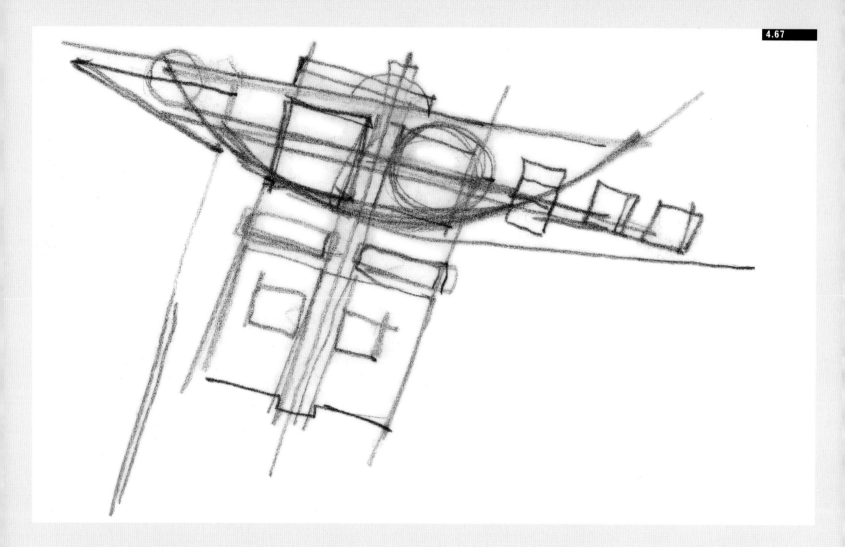

4.67

4.67
Conceptual sketch for a competition design for a new library in Copenhagen.

4.68
Sketch for the interior of a library for Selly Oak Colleges, Birmingham.

4.69
The completed library at Selly Oak Colleges was the winner of an energy conservation award.

4.68

4.69

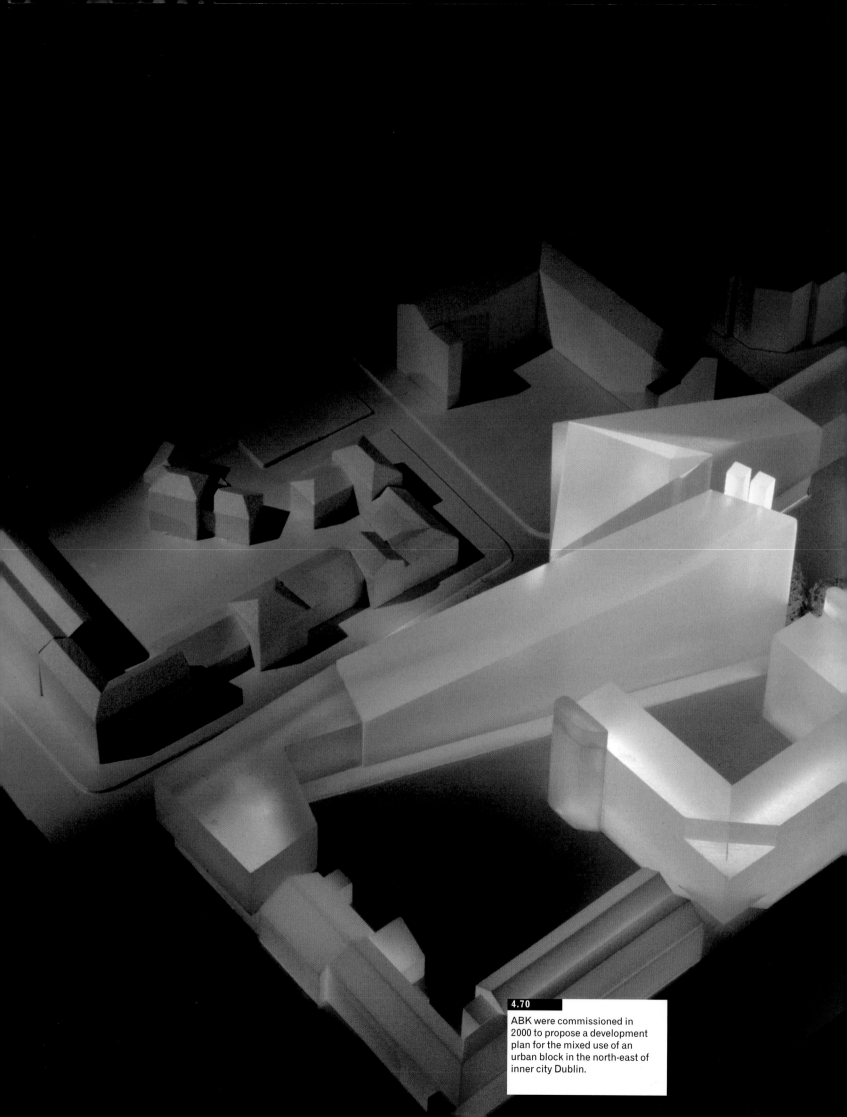

4.70
ABK were commissioned in
2000 to propose a development
plan for the mixed use of an
urban block in the north-east of
inner city Dublin.

4.70

As head of the FCO's Overseas Estate Department from 1985 to 1997, I was responsible for commissioning and briefing ABK and for guiding the project for the new British Embassy in Moscow through all of its tortuous stages.

In 1985, we held an early form of competitive interview with four practices. We thought that ABK would suit us best: they seemed the most likely to respond constructively to a brief rather than to seek to overlay upon it their own predilections, and their partners were young enough to last what proved to be a lengthy – fifteen year – commission.

It took some while for ABK to work their way into the context and to help us to develop the brief for the site on Smolenskaya, overlooking the Moscow River and close to the Russian White House. But from the outset I felt that we were working with a practice with whom we could develop a good mutual understanding. At that time there was still a need for an ultra-high security, Cold War building and the precautions required to minimise the potential for Soviet physical or technical attack were fundamental in determining the form of the building. Gradually, the outlines of a proposal developed, in external appearance, a very large monolith: between two one-sided blocks of residential accommodation running at right angles to the river was a huge void into which an almost freestanding separate building, built in UK and re-erected on the site, would be inserted.

By then, though, the Cold War was beginning to warm up and the Berlin Wall came down. Slowly it dawned that an ultra-high security solution may not in fact any longer be necessary. And so the scheme was set aside and nothing much happened for the next year or so.

The time for a radically new brief came in 1991, when it was agreed that we should move into new outline design work. I remember clearly the meeting at which the outline design was first tabled. The flats were in three blocks along the front of the site and the classified offices were in a fourth block between them. These were all raised up on a podium, with cars and plant rooms beneath, and connected by a long corridor from north to south of the site, parallel to the river. The classified offices block had an extension reaching eastwards containing the unclassified offices. Beneath this was the entrance hall and exhibition

4.71
In its final incarnation, the British Embassy consists of four buildings facing the river, one containing offices and the others providing flats for staff.

area. Where this east-west axis crossed the corridor was the crux of the site and of the design. It was a pretty clear disposition of functions and it appealed immediately. Each way that you tested something, the proposal either had an answer or an answer could readily be fitted into it. That proposal is now today's building. It naturally got more complicated as time and functional detail was piled into it, but the fundamentals of the plan were so right that we never needed to depart from them.

The design was quickly accepted by all levels in the FCO. The same could not be said of the Moscow City authorities who thought that it lacked the gravitas that an Embassy and their site demanded. Richard Burton and I made various presentations to Committees and to the Chief Architect (who, we thought, privately rather liked it). He in turn pointed out the virtues to the Mayor (who, we knew, felt it looked like holiday flats in a Black Sea resort) and eventually, after ABK had found a ways of appearing to tie the blocks together, we were rewarded with a signed and approved drawing.

As it is, however, the building is a huge success. Staff like working and living there and visitors like visiting it. The whole presents Britain in an open, forward-looking and welcoming light in Moscow.

Mark Bertram

4.71

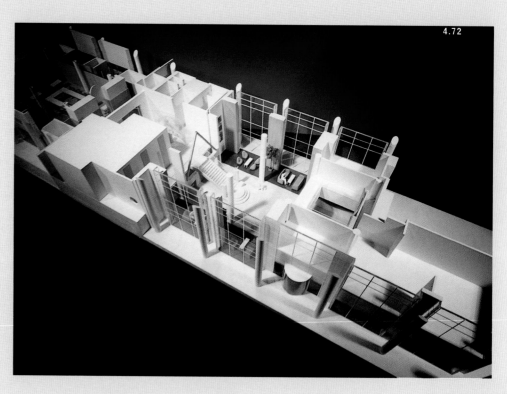

4.72

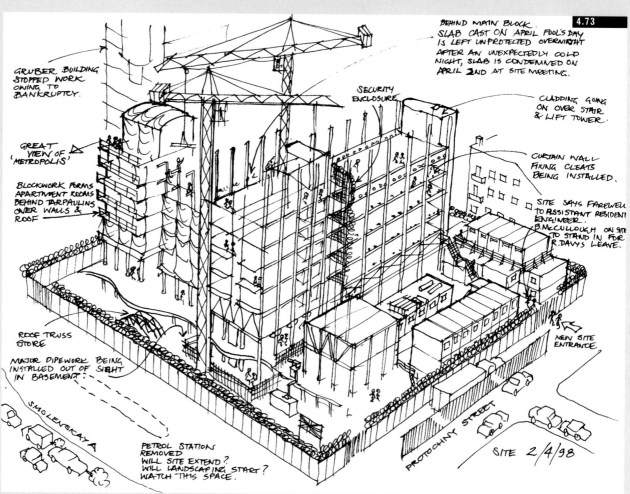

4.73

BEHIND MAIN BLOCK.
SLAB CAST ON APRIL FOOL'S DAY
IS LEFT UNPROTECTED OVERNIGHT
AFTER AN UNEXPECTEDLY COLD
NIGHT, SLAB IS CONDEMNED ON
APRIL 2ND AT SITE MEETING.

GRUBER BUILDING
STOPPED WORK
OWING TO
BANKRUPTCY.

GREAT
VIEW OF
'METROPOLIS'

BLOCKWORK FORMS
APARTMENT ROOMS
BEHIND TARPAULINS
OVER WALLS &
ROOF

ROOF TRUSS
STORE

MAJOR PIPEWORK BEING
INSTALLED OUT OF SIGHT
IN BASEMENT.

SECURITY
ENCLOSURE

CLADDING GOING
ON OVER STAIR
& LIFT TOWER.

CURTAIN WALL
FIXING CLEATS
BEING INSTALLED.

SITE SAYS FAREWELL
TO ASSISTANT RESIDENT
ENGINEER.
B.McCULLOUGH ON SITE
TO STAND IN FOR
R.DAVYS LEAVE.

NEW SITE
ENTRANCE

SMOLENSKAYA

PETROL STATION
REMOVED
WILL SITE EXTEND?
WILL LANDSCAPING START?
WATCH THIS SPACE.

PROTOCHNY STREET

SITE 2/4/98

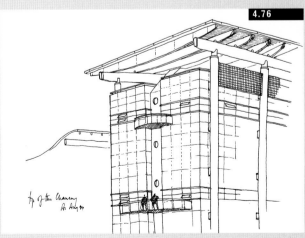

The British Embassy in progress. This study model explores the efficient use of interior spaces and the placement of works of art.

A site progress sketch, one of many by ABK's project director.

Progress on site.

Massing study. One of many considered, this drawing was made after the rebriefing in 1992.

A sketch studying materials, structure and form of the embassy's main building, its roof designed to carry the heavy weight of Moscow snowfalls.

4.77
The interior of the embassy features works by a variety of British artists, including this painting by Michael Craig-Martin.

4.78
An oblique urban view of the embassy.

4.79
Seating by Ron Arad washed with bright, low sunlight – typical of spring in Moscow.

4.80
A perspective night view of the embassy. Computer renderings played a vital role in explaining design proposals to the client.

4.81
Despite the end of the Cold War, the embassy's exterior wall is necessarily designed for security. Poetry panels add a friendly touch.

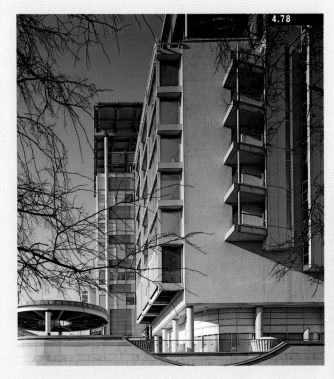

4.78

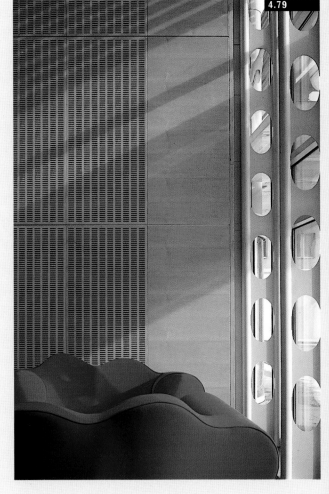

4.79

4.80

4.81

4.83

Conceptual sketch for a high
rise building on Rothschild
Boulevard, Tel Aviv. Several
options were studied for the
competition.

4.83
The winning entry for the Tel
Aviv competition. The building
occupies an important site at
the junction of two main roads.

Picture Credits

p9: © Antoine Raffoul
p10: all © John Donat
p11: © Paul Koralek
p12: top row, 1-3 courtesy of ABK, top row, 4 © John Donat, bottom: Alistair Hunter
p13: © Alistair Hunter
p14: © John Donat
p15: © Paul Koralek
p16–17: all © Paul Koralek
p18: courtesy of ABK
p19: top left: © John Donat, top right: © Martin Charles, bottom left: courtesy of ABK, bottom right: Antoine Raffoul
p20: © John Donat
p21: © John Donat
p22: top left: courtesy of ABK, top right: © John Donat, bottom left: courtesy of ABK, bottom right: © John Donat
p23: © Antoine Raffoul
p24: courtesy of ABK
p25: courtesy of ABK
p26–7: © John Donat
p28: © John Donat
p29: top: all © John Donat: bottom: courtesy of ABK
p30–1: inset left courtesy of ABK; inset right image by Hayes-Davidson; main image © John Donat
p32: © John Donat
p33: © John Donat
p34: all © John Donat
p35: all © John Donat
p36: all © Peter Cook/View
p37: © Peter Cook/View
p38–9: © Martin Charles
p40–1: © John Donat
p42–3: top row 1, 2 © John

Donat; 3, 4 courtesy of ABK, bottom row: 1 © John Donat; 2 © Chris Gascoigne; 3 © Robert Greshoff; 4 courtesy of ABK
p44–5: main image © James Morris, inset Aerofilms Ltd, London
p46: top row 1, 2 courtesy of ABK; 3 Antoine Raffoul; bottom row: all courtesy of ABK
p47: courtesy of ABK
p48: © Peter Cook/View
p49: all courtesy of ABK
p50: 1, 2 courtesy of ABK; 3, 4 Paul Koralek
p52: left: © Norman McGrath: right: © Keith Reynolds
p53: © Norman McGrath
p54: top row 1, 2 courtesy of ABK; 3 Antoine Raffoul; 4 courtesy of ABK; bottom © Martin Charles
p55: © The Times
p56: © John Donat
p57: left © Aerofilms Ltd; top right © Martin Charles; bottom right courtesy of ABK
p58: © John Donat
p59: top row 1,2: © Martin Charles; 3 © John Donat; 4 © Martin Charles; bottom © John Donat
p60: all courtesy of ABK
p61: courtesy Civic Trust Awards
p62: © John Donat
p63: © John Donat
p64: top row 1, 2 Antoine Raffoul; 3 © John Donat, bottom © John Donat all courtesy of ABK
p66: top row: courtesy of ABK
p67: top left courtesy of ABK; top right © Antoine Raffoul; bottom left courtesy of ABK; bottom

right © B Bulley
p68–9: courtesy of ABK
p70: top row 1, 2, 3 © John Donat; bottom left M Bradley; bottom right courtesy of ABK
p71: © John Donat
p72: top row 1, 2 courtesy of ABK; 3 © John Donat; 4 © M Antrobus; bottom row all courtesy of ABK
p73: © Paul Koralek
p74: © John Donat
p75: top row all © John Donat; bottom left courtesy of ABK; bottom right © Martin Charles
p76–7: © Martin Charles
p78: all courtesy of ABK
p79: courtesy of ABK
p80: all courtesy of ABK
p81: courtesy of ABK
p82–3: © Peter Cook/View
p84–5: inset images © John Donat; main image © Peter Cook/View
p86: all courtesy of ABK
p87: courtesy of ABK
p88–9: courtesy of ABK
p90: © Norman McGrath
p91: © John Donat
p92–3: © Martin Charles
p94: courtesy of ABK
p95 : inset courtesy of ABK; main image © Walter Rawlings
p96: © Chris Gascoigne
p97: © Ove Arup and Partners
p98: courtesy of ABK
p99: all courtesy of ABK
p100: bottom left © John Donat; all others courtesy of ABK
p101: © John Donat
p102: courtesy of ABK
p103: left © John Donat; right © Martin Charles

p104–5: © John Donat
p106–7: courtesy of ABK
p108: courtesy of ABK
p109: top row 1, 2 courtesy of ABK, 3 © Charlotte Wood; bottom row all courtesy of ABK
p110–1: © Paul Koralek
p112: © John Donat
p113: © John Donat
p114–5: © Paul Koralek
p116: © Martin Charles
p117: courtesy of ABK
p118: © Dennis Gilbert
p119: © John Donat
p120: courtesy of ABK
p121: © John Donat
p122–3: main image © John Donat; inset images 1–4 © John Donat
p124: all © Peter Cook/View
p125: © Peter Cook/View
p126: © John Donat
p127: all © Peter Cook/View
p128: all courtesy of ABK
p129: all courtesy of ABK
p130 : all courtesy of ABK
p131: all courtesy of ABK
p132: Top: © Peter Cook/View; bottom courtesy of ABK
p133: © Peter Cook/View
p134: courtesy of ABK
p135: all courtesy of ABK
p136: all courtesy of ABK
p137: all courtesy of ABK
p138: courtesy of ABK
p139: left courtesy of ABK; right © Peter Cook/View
p140: top left, right courtesy of ABK; bottom left, right © Dennis Gilbert
p141: all courtesy of ABK
p142–3: all courtesy of ABK
p144: all courtesy of ABK.

p145: Left © Peter Cook/View; top right © Charlotte Wood; bottom right © Peter Cook/View;
p146: top left © John Donat; bottom left © M Coverright courtesy of ABK
p147: © Martin Charles
p148–9: © C Edgecombe
p150: all courtesy of ABK
p151: left and bottom right © John Donat; top right: courtesy of ABK
p152: all courtesy of ABK
p153: courtesy of ABK
p154: top left courtesy of ABK; top right © Peter Cook/View; bottom left, right courtesy of ABK
p155: all courtesy of ABK
p156: all courtesy of ABK
p157: all courtesy of ABK
p158–9: main image courtesy of ABK; inset © John Donat
p160: all courtesy of ABK
p161: all courtesy of ABK; right © Paul Koralek
p162–3: courtesy of ABK
p164–5: © Peter Cook/View
p166: all courtesy of ABK
p167: all courtesy of ABK
p168: © Peter Cook/View
p169: top left © Peter Cook/View; top right: courtesy of ABK; bottom left © Peter Cook/View; bottom right © Peter Cook/View
p170: courtesy of ABK
p171: courtesy of ABK

Project Index

Page numbers in italics refer to projects included in visual essays; roman script refers to projects mentioned in text essays

Publisher's Acknowledgements:

Sheena Cruse, Catherine Ford, Marit Münzberg, Monika Fink, Raj Manickavasagam, Lise Connellan, Anthony Barley, Christopher Brawn, Robert Steiger, Nicole Liniger, Kate Trant, Marjorie Allthorpe-Guyton, Kenneth Powell, and especially Peter Ahrends, Richard Burton, Paul Koralek, David Cruse and their colleagues at ABK

The publishers and ABK wish to thank the following organisations for their support which has made this publication possible:

Arts Council of England
ARUP
ARUP Consulting Engineers
Buro Happold
Northcroft
Patterson Kempster and Shortall
Samuely
Allgood Worldwide Limited
Blanc de Bierges – Milner Delvaux Ltd
Velfac Ltd
RIBA Journal
Architects' Journal

Further information about ABK can be found on the practice's web site: www.abk.co.uk
Email address:
abk@abklondon.com

About the authors:

Paul Finch is publishing director of *the Architects' Journal* and the *Architectural Review*. He edited *AJ* from 1994 until September 1999. He was a member of the DETR's Advisory Group for the Greater London Authority Headquarters and contributes to a wide range of forums as a commentator on architecture and design. He is deputy chairman of the Commission for Architecture and the Built Environment, and chairs its Design Review Committee.

Elain Harwood is an architectural historian specialising in the postwar era. She is an Inspector of Buildings for English Heritage and is a regular convenor of seminars on the subject of postwar architecture. She has written or contributed to a number of publications including *Preserving Postwar Heritage* (English Heritage); *England: a guide to postwar listed buildings* (Ellipsis); *Tayler and Green Architects* (with Alan Powers, Prince of Wales's Institute of Architecture), *London, Exploring England's Heritage* (Stationery Office) and most recently *Twentieth Century Architecture 5: Festival of Britain* (Twentieth Century Society).

Frank McDonald is Environment Editor of the *Irish Times*, having served as Environment Correspondent from 1986. He is the author of *The Destruction of Dublin* (Gill and Macmillan) and *Saving the City* (Tomar), two books which helped to change public policy on urban renewal, as well as *The Construction of Dublin* (Gandon Editions). He is also a director of Energy Action, a charity which tackles fuel poverty among the elderly.

Jeremy Melvin is an architectural historian whose books include *Young British Architects* (Birkhäuser) and a forthcoming monograph on FRS Yorke (Thames and Hudson). He has contributed to other books and numerous professional, national and international publications. He teaches at South Bank University and is a consultant to the Royal Academy for its architecture programme.

Kenneth Powell is an architecture writer whose books include *Richard Rogers Complete Works* (Phaidon, two volumes), *City Transformed* (Laurence King), *Structure Space and Skin* (Phaidon), *Will Alsop* (Laurence King) and *New London Architecture* (Merrell). Forthcoming books include a second volume on the work of Will Alsop. He is a regular contributor to a number of magazines including *Architects' Journal* and was formerly architecture correspondent of the *Daily Telegraph*. He is consultant director of the Twentieth Century Society.